# THY KINGDOM COME

# PART 4

## FROM HERE TO ETERNITY

## Beryl Moore

SERVING THE KING

SOVEREIGN MINISTRIES
BERYL MOORE

Formatted by Freedom Publishing
Cover by Esther Kotecha, EKDesign
Printed in the United Kingdom

# Contents

## Section 1 - Mind the Gap

# Section 2 - His Majesty

# Section 3 - Experiencing God

Many Christians would admit that there is at least one thing missing in their current experience of Christianity; the question *'Is that all there is?'* could be hovering unspoken on their lips.

This, the fourth and last volume in the series, addresses a missing piece -- that is - we are a *heavenly* people; a nation on the earth set apart for God; to *reflect* heaven on earth and to *bring* heaven to earth by virtue of the fact that we are in the world at this time though not of it; we are characterised by our peace and rest in every situation.

We are here, *for* a time such as this.

A radical approach, maybe, but the scriptures are quite clear; God called Israel to be His own; when she refused, He turned to the Gentile nations to prepare a Bride for His Son, one who would love Him and be exactly like Him, fulfilling His plan from before the foundation of the earth, a people for Himself.

But to reign and rule with Him for eternity, His bride must be fully compatible with Him; she must be like Him, think like Him, act like Him, perceive as He does…

As the Bride emerges in the early years of the 21$^{st}$ century, her single focus is her Bridegroom; she only has eyes for Him – and that maybe, is yet another missing piece…perhaps even another book.

Enter then, into the power of resurrection life; a life that expresses the desire of heaven as we say as Jesus Himself taught us, *"Father, Thy Kingdom come, Thy will be done in **me** on earth, as I train to reign and rule with your Beloved Son for eternity".* Amen. (Matthew 6:10 KJV)

# The Rest of Faith

*"There still exists, therefore, a full and complete rest for the people of God." (Hebrews 4:9 Phillips)*

"I am sure it will sound to many of you like going a long way back and going out into a very broad realm when I say that we Christians are being constantly confronted with and challenged by our Christianity.

Many of us have not really entered into Christianity yet. What do I mean? Well, for one thing, the very door into true Christianity is the door of rest, the rest of faith. The very simple way in which the Lord put it in His appeal was – *"Come unto Me, all ye that labour and are heavy laden, and I will give you rest"* (Matthew 11:28 KJV). That was to a multitude, and those words are usually employed in Gospel messages to the unsaved.

The meaning of the Lord in using those words is given to us here in the letter to the Hebrews, a very much deeper and fuller meaning than is generally recognized in the usage of the simple invitation *"Come unto Me... and I will give you rest."* There is something that we have to hear, to detect, in the statement – *"There remains therefore a sabbath rest for the people of God"* (Hebrews 4:9 ASV).

You will not think me too elementary, for you know in your heart as well as I do in mine, that this matter of heart rest; the rest of faith; is a live question continually, it is coming up all the time. One of the things which is lacking in so many of us is this rest, or, to put it the other way, the things which characterize us so much are fret, anxiety, uncertainty, and all those things which are just the opposite of calm assurance, quiet confidence, the spirit, and atmosphere which says all the time, 'Don't worry, don't fret, it is all right'. One thing our great enemy is always trying to do is to disturb that, destroy that, rob us of that, churn us up, fret us, drive us, harass us, anything to rob us of our rest or to prevent us from entering into rest.

It is the rest *of faith*, not just the rest of passivity, indifference, and carelessness. There is all the difference between carelessness and carefreeness.

There remains, there is still to be had, there still obtains, there still exists, there is still preserved, a rest for the people of God – for *the people of God.*"

T. Austin-Sparks from: The Rest and Courage of Faith. Daily Windows, subscribed, Austin-Sparks.net.

# Foreword

As we embark on the final leg of our journey through the Sermon on the Mount, Matthew chapters 5,6 and 7, we see clearly that we really are no longer earthly people, but heavenly, spiritual, beings; more glorious than we know, stronger than we look, more beautiful than we can imagine, and that God plans for eternity.

It is as we appropriate *everything* Jesus won for us on the Cross, we truly become the people He died for, the glorious Bride He longs for, the one that satisfies His heart; and we begin to comprehend just how great a salvation He won for us.

When we speak of glory, we mean the goodness and supernatural power of Jesus Christ.

We can only learn Who Jesus is by coming up against situations in our lives that are, in the natural totally impossible, because *this* is where His glory is shown; when He moves *supernaturally* on our behalf, we become a people who see the invisible and believe the impossible, a bride fit for the King.

If you haven't done so already then, be prepared to move your feet and discover for yourself how *great* a salvation you really, really, have as you fully enter into the inheritance set aside for you from the foundation of the earth, so that you might indeed rule and reign with your Lord for *eternity,* starting now because you are already in resurrection life...Enjoy.

# Section 1

## Mind The Gap

*"He labours most abundantly who realises most fully that he is a stranger and pilgrim on earth, that he is not a citizen of time, but that eternity is his home, that God is his portion."*

Adolph Saphir, 'The Hidden Life', p 56 Forgotten Books 2015

# 1

# Convergence

Everything converges at this point.

We have looked at the Sermon on the Mount and what Jesus tells us is our pattern for living, our paradigm for life, as new creations who stand on resurrection ground.

We discovered we had some basic misunderstandings, which we looked at last time, setting ourselves the right way up.

Now we need to look at the **normal** Christian life as envisaged by Jesus; the glory of the Cross; living in resurrection life and our **experience** of God.

The life of abiding in the Vine; no longer growing from the old stock of our fallen Adamic nature, but in vital living union with the True Vine; grafted in, growing, and bearing abundant fruit -

*"I am the true vine, and My Father is the vinedresser. Every branch in Me that does not bear fruit He takes away; and every branch that bears fruit He prunes, that it may bear more fruit. You are already clean because of the word which I have spoken to you. Abide in Me, and I in you. As the branch cannot bear fruit of itself, unless it abides in the vine, neither can you, unless you abide in Me."* (John 15:1-4 NKJV)

God wills that we know Him; experience Him; and abide in Him, above all else, because without Him - we can do nothing -

*"Eternal life means to know and experience you as the only true God, and to **know and experience** Jesus Christ, as the Son whom you have sent."* (Emphasis mine) (John 17:3)

If we have seen anything in our journey so far, it is that He desires we have a vibrant, living, and personal relationship with Him. He wants us to **know Him and experience Him**, not just know about Him –

I want you to know Me,
Know My holiness
Know My perfection
Know My joy
Know My love
Know My goodness
Know My plans
Know Me,
Know
Me,
Know
My desire -
towards you.

Herein lies the rub.

Many of us are happy to learn all manner of facts and figures about the Christ, but back off when the issue of *intimacy* with Him comes to the fore.

If this is you beloved, recognise here and now you were created for an eternal love relationship with your Creator.

Eternal life, resurrection power, rest and peace are your inheritance and your portion.

He will not rest Himself until you *know* and *experience* Him in His fulness; not just know about Him, which is measure.

So, at the start of this session maybe you have some decisions to make - remember, decisions determine destiny; attitudes determine altitude, and life in the Spirit is about displacement.

He is a God who delights to reveal Himself and does so increasingly from Genesis to Revelation.

Having revealed Himself, He shows you what He sees when He looks at you and the glorious future, He has planned for you.

The only fly in the ointment, if I can use that phrase, is you and your willingness, or not, to follow His plan for your life, not yours.

God cannot, if man will not.

# 2

# God Wills

So, God **wills** that you know Him, not just know about Him.

He desires that you experience Him and come into alignment with His plan for your life.

Every time He reveals something to you about His eternal nature and Godhead, He will want to make that real to you in your own personal experience; so, you will receive a revelation, which will be followed by an experience of what He has just shown you of Himself.

For instance, you may have a financial lack, which He has promised to fill; when He does so, you will know Him as your provider; you will not just have an academic understanding, you will have *experienced* Him as this.

You will *know* that the Lord is your Shepherd, and you will lack nothing - by experience. (cf Psalm 23 NIV)

He loves to make things real in this way. He loves to back everything up He reveals of Himself, with an experience.

To make the most of this you will need to understand His ways with you, and the principles upon which He works.

The children of Israel knew His works; Moses knew His ways. (cf Psalm 103:7 NIV).

The children of Israel walked continuously after their own will and way, which resulted in their being where they are right now, set aside for a season, until the full number of Gentiles - that's us - has come in.

His intention was always that they should occupy a land of milk and honey, the Promised Land, where they could grow, settle, and thrive. They never made it, the fault was not on God's side, but theirs. God is faithful, He hasn't finished with them, and we can learn so much about how He likes to do things by studying where they went wrong, seeing God's faithfulness to them, and ensuring that we don't make the same mistakes they did.

Remember it is possible to drink from the river and die in the wilderness...they did.

So, maybe the first thing we need to get straight is that God plans for eternity, from eternity.

He has no afterthoughts.

Everything is complete and finished in His eyes.

There isn't a plan 'B'.

Just so you know...

He doesn't just formulate a plan for your life the moment you believe.

You are *not* an afterthought.

You have been in His plan and His heart from before the foundation of the earth.

God *chose* you way back then.

He *called* you according to the good pleasure of *His* will.

He has a *plan* for your life.

A good one.

He makes this known to you, then He develops you, after His pattern, to fulfil the destiny He has already written for you as He has purposed in His great heart.

It's all Him.

It's all GOOD.

Your part is simply to believe and co-operate.

He takes us through a circle, a cycle, a process of sonship; servanthood; friendship and finally, ruined for anything else, we become His utter, drooling, love slave and partner.

He establishes us as His children first and foremost always, and when He is satisfied we are secure in this, He moves us round to learn to serve for a season; next step is we are called into friendship; and finally, when our heart is totally captivated by Him - we become His love slave.

You don't go round this circle or cycle just once, but many, many, times during your Christian life and walk, and in different areas of your life, so it makes sense to find out where you are right now in order that you can fully co-operate with Him in whatever experience He wants you to have.

Why not take a moment out right now to find out just where you are in this cycle; if you aren't sure, just ask Him, He is *so* willing to tell you.

# 3

# That you might know Me

Right at the front end, we need to **believe** that He is good; that He is for us, He is not against us; and His goodness extends not only towards us, as His children, but to everybody else; the good, the bad and the ugly - to the Hitler's, the Bin Laden's, the Satanists...we are not living in a season of judgement, but of Grace - amazing Grace – the **Grace** of our Lord Jesus Christ – God is **GOOD**, He's **GOOD**...**He's <u>very</u> GOOD**...He told us so -

*"I Myself will make all My **goodness** pass before you, and will proclaim the name of the LORD before you; and I will be gracious to whom I will be gracious, and will show compassion on whom I will show compassion."* (Exodus 33:19 NASB)

The goodness of God encompasses so many things; it says He is compassionate, gracious, cordial, pleasant, affable, genial, friendly, and warm. He is amiable, approachable, thoughtful, convivial, and cheerful. He is kind, benevolent and full of goodwill towards all men. He is slow to anger, and abundant in loving-kindness and mercy.

He is tenderhearted and quick in both understanding and empathy towards us; He is open, frank, and friendly, He is joyful, playful, and He desires to reveal Himself in all His glory towards anyone who is even halfway interested to know Him. Notwithstanding all that, He is inclined always to bless, and He takes great pleasure in His people.

He has promised that He Himself is our inheritance...everything He is and has, is ours, and we are His, the people of His inheritance.

And bonus, He isn't revolted by our wretchedness; He doesn't despise us in our intransigence and weakness, our foolishness, or our deceitfulness. He loves us 100% all the way, all the time, no matter what; and He always has.

His love is not dependent upon our performance but flows out towards that upon which He has set His affection – this is His decision, He **chose** to put His love upon us, it does not depend upon our performance...upon us getting it 'right'.

And He wills that we are as full of joy as He is, that we belong to Him, and out of His goodness, He sees us perfected in the Beloved; because it pleased Him to bruise Jesus that we might have an eternal inheritance **in** Him.

His wrath was **fully** spent on Jesus on the cross. He is no longer angry, he is no longer vengeful; Jesus has taken all the punishment in His own body on the tree.

He is unceasingly magnificent towards us.

Towards you.

You heard that right, beloved, *you.*

This is what He planned from before the foundation of the earth – a people for Himself who would know Him and freely love Him; **desire** Him, **know** Him and **enjoy** Him.

He desires, to be –

Known -

*I want you to know Me,*

*Know My holiness*
*Know My perfection*
*Know My joy*
*Know My love*
*Know My goodness*
*Know My plans*
*Know Me*
*Know Me*
*I want you to know*

*Me.*

And I have given you My Holy Spirit for this express purpose that you might know Me; and become more and more intimately acquainted with Me.

You have everything you need, beloved, everything for a life of power, peace and rest.

So, what are you waiting for?

# 4

# Genesis to Revelation

Continuing our theme, the bible shows God's self-revelation from Genesis to Revelation.

He revealed Himself to Adam as the LORD God – Jehovah Elohim, the Most Powerful of all the powerful ones – Creator and final authority over man.

To Abram, chosen father of the nation of Israel – He revealed Himself as a Covenant Maker and Covenant Keeper – the One who reckons not on our weakness but on His strength; the God Who compels nature to do what is contrary to itself – Sarai found that out and became Sarah – mother and Princess.

To Moses, chosen deliverer of a nation – He revealed Himself as 'I AM' – the Self-Existent One – Whose Presence, He promised, would go with Moses.

To the Jewish nation – He revealed Himself as Messiah – long awaited Saviour, Deliverer and King.

To us, the Gentiles, He reveals Himself as - Saviour, Lord, Deliverer, Bridegroom, Lover, coming Warrior King and Judge – accepted by some rejected by others.

He has *always* revealed Himself to man – culminating in that great and eternal Revelation of His Nature and Glory in the book of the same name – read it sometime if you want to improve your devotional life.

This great God, who lays out the heavens in all their glory, Who is constantly creating more galaxies just for the fun of it; to Whom every night is firework night; delights to progressively reveal Himself to His creation...and stoops to conquer our hearts in order that He might have a people for Himself.

This is how He is and has always been; He is not a God who hides Himself from us and He never, ever changes – He is immutable, and He is infinite – what He is He always was and always will be. He always has been good, and He always will be good, because He cannot change the way He is He is unchanging, immutable.

What He was, He is and always will be – He is Good...

The Self-Existent One – I AM.

He is immutable, and He is *good*.

Forever.

Infinitely.

Eternally.

And He will always be - *exactly like this*.

# 5

# He is in pursuit

For me the Gospel is encapsulated in -

*"Eternal life means to know and experience you
as the only true God,
and to know and experience Jesus Christ,
as the Son whom you have sent."* (John 17:3)

To know Him **and** experience Him.

You can know *of* someone, or even live with someone, but never really **know** him or her; I lived with my husband for 25 years, but I never really *knew* him.

You can have known *of* Jesus and God the Father for sixty years, and still not know or experience either of them.

Sobering thought really, but the Spirit is saying, *"this year is the year I want you to experience Me in all My glory, I want you to experience for yourself, what I am for you…"*

*"What I am for you"* - not the other fellow - **you**.

Up front and personal, you are cornered.

He is coming after *you* with romantic intent.

You will no longer be able to resist Him or hold Him at arm's length, because He, is coming after **you**.

*"Still, still, without ceasing, I feel it increasing, this fervour of holy desire and often exclaim let me die in the flame, of a love that can never expire..."*[1]

You are cornered beloved, cornered.

You now have a choice – fight, flee or submit; lay down your arms in surrender.

Either way He isn't going to let you go.

He is **so** intentional in His pursuit of you.

Like a bridegroom pursuing His bride...

Which of course, is what He is...in pursuit of His Bride.

[1] *'The Christian book of Mystical' Verse*, A. W. Tozer, Madame Jeanne Guyon, poem *'The fervour of holy desire'* p.53. Martino Publishing 2010.

# 6

# He calls us to Himself

Some years ago, at least ten maybe fifteen, the Lord said to me on the eve of a New Year, *"tell my Bride – "Coming, ready or not"".*

It all brings us back to the restoration of the Creator creature relationship.

From us telling Him what to do and what we want, to Him reaching down and saying -

*"Let My people go that they might worship Me".* (Exodus 8:1 NIV)

When He begins to restore and revive His people, it always starts with their return to Him -

*"So Moses and Aaron went to Pharaoh and said to him, "This is what the Lord, the God of the Hebrews, says: 'How long will you refuse to humble yourself before me? Let my people go, so that they may worship me.'""* (Exodus 10: 3 NIV)

He doesn't call us to ministry or service, but to Himself...that we might worship

**Him.**

Get things back the right way up.

Honour *Him*, love *Him*, obey *Him* - because of Who He is. Gone are the days when we could call Him *'the Man upstairs'* or *'The Guvnor'* and not feel uncomfortable, because these sayings show immediately, we *do not* know Him; we are not in a living, vital relationship with Him, because we neither love nor respect Him.

If we did, our love would constrain us from speaking in such a way.

As would our respect.

When you love someone, you cannot use loose, derogatory terms about him or her.

He is restoring His holiness, righteousness, and awe of Who He is to His people, and we do well to hear what the Spirit is saying to the churches right now because whom the Lord loves, He corrects -

*"And have you forgotten his encouraging words spoken to you as his children? He said,*

*"My child, don't underestimate the value*
*of the discipline and training of the Lord God,*
*or get depressed when he has to correct you.*
*For the Lord's training of your life*
*is the evidence of his faithful love.*
*And when he draws you to himself,*
*it proves you are his delightful child."*

*Fully embrace God's correction as part of your training, for he is doing what any loving father does for his children. For who has ever heard of a child who never had to be corrected?"* (Hebrews 12:5-7)

We are still getting things the right way up and it all starts with how we see Him and moves to whether we will accept correction or not...

How do you do on the correction front?

Just a question…observer, objector, resister, responder?

Nailed?

What we *think* about Him is the single most important thing in our lives.

I'll repeat that statement, what we think about God is **the** single most important thing in our lives.

It drives all we are and everything we do.

The Kingdom *within* you will always focus on the new man in Christ; the saving power of Jesus; the anointing of the Holy Spirit; and the passion of the Father for you to inherit everything He has planned for you.

It will influence your thinking, seeing, and speaking.

Jesus wants us to be *Kingdom* people; He came to establish His Kingship and His Kingdom; first in us; then through us.

He wants His Kingdom to come here on the earth *through* us, we are His representatives, His ambassadors.

He wants us to *participate* in everything He won for us on the Cross; to *unlearn* everything we think we know and discover the royal law of love and what it means, really means, to belong to Him; to exist for Him alone; and to live out our lives on the earth as a visual aid; a demonstration of the intimate relationship we have with our Creator, and His love for His creation.

I have called this session *'Mind the gap'* because again I sense we are finding that there still is one - gap that is - between our understanding of what it means to be in Christ, and what He wants us to know, experience and enjoy.

Off we go again then.

Please fasten your seat belts; we are about to make a swift ascent and this time we *are* flying the right way up.

# 7

# Trains of thought

Trains of thought; they show up another gap between the way we think and the way He does. I don't know about you, but I get them, trains of thought...

Right now, I am running with two - the fact of our iniquities, transgressions and sin and covenants.

How do they tie up?

In my mind, our iniquities, transgressions, and sin are *all* dealt with in the New Covenant made in Jesus' blood.

He took **every** sin mankind has ever committed or would commit and nailed them to the Cross when He died there; where, incidentally, we were nailed also.

That doesn't mean that now we no longer fail, fall, or get it wrong, what it does mean is that in His covenant love, His absolute supreme, signed in His own blood covenant of love, we are not made to feel guilty about our lack or failure, but are loved and honoured, and lifted out of our mess by His Almighty power.

The bible uses several categories to describe missing the mark of God's standard of righteousness. The Hebrew language has words each with its own specific meaning: -

1) Chata, "sin", – falling short; an error, a failure, missing of the mark – it was an archery term for missing the target.

2) Pesha, "trespass", something done out of rebelliousness deliberately.

3) Aveira - "transgression". This is stepping over God's stated line: again, a deliberate act breaking God's laws and rules; a flouting of His authority.

4) Avone, "iniquity", a sin committed out of moral failing or weakness. Iniquity usually describes wickedness.

We all stumble and fall; we all experience failure and sin; but His covenant love protects us, and watches over us, even when we are right in the middle of our mess whether it is deliberate or not.

As God said to a friend once, when he was being deliberately difficult and knew it; *"Live with it, it's Who I am; I'm big enough and lovely enough to cover all your puny efforts to be more obnoxious than normal!"*

How lovely is that?

He knows us, and He loves us, just where we are, and He's not about to leave us there. He *never* throws the baby out with the bathwater!

He has planted deep inside every believer a new **godly** will that doesn't want to sin and never agrees to it (1 John 3:9 NIV) but there is also still within, a **will** belonging to our fallen, lower nature which cannot desire to do anything that isn't low or self-centred – darn it.

He sees these two natures constantly, and He sees the war that rages within us; as someone has said, Satan pulling one leg and Jesus pulling the other and it depends on who wins on any given day.

God is moved with *great* compassion towards us in our struggle to choose that which is right, over that which our lower nature desires, and by His Spirit He constantly moves to help us.

Every sin that we commit against someone else is simply the result of not knowing the covenant love in which we ourselves are safely and securely held.
Our lower nature just doesn't comprehend how much God loves it, or it would see those around in a completely different light.

We live in darkness and selfish fear, protecting ourselves against each other, when He is trying to release us fully into knowing and being known.

Everything comes down to this, our lack of *knowing* just how much we are totally loved, accepted, and approved.

Just how utterly supernatural our rebirth was, that put us on heavenly, resurrection, ground.

He cannot be untrue to Himself.

He has covenanted to love us.

Makes you think, doesn't it? It makes me think anyway and it makes me very, very grateful for His great love and unending grace towards me on my worst day…

Mind the gap.

# 8

# He is good

Let's take a look at your idea of God for a moment.

What is His character?

What sort of God is He to you?

If we believe at the outset that He is good, then there is no second cause to anything.

If He has allowed something to come to you, it must be for your growth, profit, increase, training, equipping, upgrade and ultimate good. Ask Job.

**All** things, the good, the bad and the ugly He allows into our lives, are for our ultimate good; and because He is good, He cannot do bad things.

But He does allow in His wisdom what He could easily prevent by His power.

Julian of Norwich would put it this way –

*"All the power of our enemy is shut up in the hand of our Friend."*[1]

That makes thanksgiving, praise and rejoicing a way of life for us – heads we win, tails we win – we fight *from* victory, not towards it; God is for us, not against us. We are His inheritance, and He is ours. Yahoo!

He, and He alone, is our exceeding great reward, and He Himself is our rest.

Knowing God, as our inheritance, is to understand and believe that everything we lack, is made up for us in the Christ.

He died and rose again that we would *inherit* all that He is and all that He can do; and, bonus, nothing can come at us unless He sovereignly allows it.

We simply cannot lose.

We are in Him and He is in us, and He is in the Father, we are double wrapped '*Christ in you the hope of glory...*' (Colossians 1:27 NIV)

We are **kept** by the power of God.

All our circumstances are designed to enable us to be established in our faith and to be overflowing with gratitude.

Overflowing with gratitude – that'll be us.

When we know Who He is; who we are in Him; and what His intentions are towards us; we cannot help but overflow with gratitude –


*"Eye has not seen nor ear heard, nor have entered into the heart of man, what God has prepared for those who love Him".* (1 Corinthians 2:9 NKJV)


He is **Good**.

And He has good plans for us.

We were created **by** Him for fellowship **with** Him.

We are to be conformed to His image.

And He wants us to **know** Him, not just know about Him.

He wants us to know by experience and believe that He is good, no matter how the world shakes us up and spins us round; or what our circumstances (or others), are saying.

How often in our ignorance and anger, though, do we secretly blame Him as the first cause of our difficulties - and shake our fist?

Be honest now, haven't you felt like that at times when something bad has happened; in your deepest heart you held **Him** responsible for it –

*"Why did You allow this to happen? I thought You loved me…"*

Maybe you still hold Him in unforgiveness?

A W Tozer, In this most beautiful prayer, expresses Him *'unblamed'* -

*"O Lord God Almighty, not the God of the philosophers and the wise, but the God of the prophets and apostles; and better than all, the God and Father of our Lord Jesus Christ, may I express Thee unblamed? They that know Thee not may call upon Thee as other than Thou art, and so worship not Thee but a creature of their own fancy; therefore enlighten our minds that we may know Thee as Thou art, so that we may perfectly love Thee and worthily praise Thee, in the name of Jesus Christ our Lord. Amen."* [2]

Do you need to forgive God where you have held Him responsible?

Now there's a thought and maybe even a prayer for you today.

[1] 'I Promise you a Crown' Julian of Norwich, David Hazard, Bethany House Publishers, 1995, page 12.
[2] 'The Knowledge of the Holy' A W Tozer, Harper San Francisco, 1978 p.1

# 9

# Our Chief End

The Westminster Catechism first asks us a question, and then answers it for us

*"What is the chief end of man? The chief end of man is to glorify God and enjoy Him forever. That which he should seek after as His chief happiness"*[1]

In that statement we have two very important ideas - our chief end is to **glorify God** – not rail at Him - which means to denounce, protest against, or attack somebody or something in bitter or harsh language. And that we should seek after **Him** as our **chief happiness**, that we should desire Him above all else.

I feel another gap coming on.

Glorify Him as God, yes, but the chief end of my happiness…you are joking?

That God should be the source of our **chief happiness** is maybe something we hadn't previously thought about.

So, maybe we need to - think about it a little, that is.

It's a bit like the first commandment, you remember that – *"You shall love the Lord your God with all your heart, with all your soul, with all your mind and with all your strength";* (Luke 10:27 NKJV) Jesus speaking.

What if God is asking us in these days to simply put the first commandment first?

What if He is asking us to make **Him** the object of our affections our chief happiness - our highest goal, our passion? Not your family, your job, your house, your car, money, your dog, but Him…

Passion.

God feels passion.

He is passionate over you; His Bride; He's passionate about mankind…but -

*"The most revealing thing about the church is her idea of God, just as her most significant message is what she says about Him, or leaves unsaid, for her silence is often more significant than her speech. She can never escape the self-disclosure of her witness concerning God."*[2]

Ouch.

What is your personal picture of God?

What do you disclose of Him in your witness to Him?

When people talk to you, what do they receive of your knowledge of Him, how you see Him?

What's your passion?

*"I am the Lord your God, who brought you out of the land of Egypt, out of the house of slavery. "You shall have no other gods before Me. "You shall not make for yourself an idol, or any likeness of what is in heaven above or on the earth beneath or in the water under the earth." (Exodus 20:2–4 NASB)*

*You shall have no other gods before **Me**…*

Other gods…

Idolatry.

In the church?

In the 21$^{st}$ century?

Idolatry; hero worship, adoration, veneration; anything that fills the spot He should occupy – your job, your spouse, your car, clothes, your house, your dog; yourself, your football team; me myself and I; fill in your own blanks.

You can easily establish what yours is; it's what you make an idol of - it is what fills your mind continuously; it is what you spend your money on; what you love; where your heart rests; the default position of your mind, what you think most about.

And beloved, idolatry is also the entertainment of thoughts about God that are unworthy of Him; because what you think about Him *is* the most important thing in your life – the idolater imagines things about God and then acts as though they are true…

Paul talked about it -

*"Casting down arguments and every high thing that exalts itself against the knowledge of God, bringing every thought into captivity to the obedience of Christ".* (2 Corinthians 10:5 NKJV)

Always the most revealing thing about the church corporately and as individuals, is her *idea* of God. How we think of Him is how we will portray Him to those around us -

*"It is impossible to keep our moral practices sound and our inward attitudes right while our idea of God is erroneous or inadequate. If we would bring back spiritual power to our lives, we must begin to think of God more nearly as He is…*[3]

*It is my opinion that the Christian conception of God current in these middle years of the twentieth century is so decadent as to be utterly beneath the dignity of the Most High God and actually to constitute for professed believers something amounting to a moral calamity…*[4]

Our conception *'so decadent as to be utterly beneath the dignity of the Most High God'* - that's painful to hear.

But it could be convicting also.

Maybe we need to revise our thoughts about Him today.

Because that gap's opening up again.

---

[1] Westminster Catechism
[2] A W Tozer, *'The Knowledge of the Holy'* page 1. Harper San Francisco, 1978.

[3] Ibid preface p viii.

[4] Ibid, p 2.

# 10

# He never changes

As the goodness and love of God is the driving force behind everything He does and all the blessings He daily bestows, He cannot be anything other than the way He is. He is immutable, He never, ever, changes. His immutability is probably the attribute I love the most. I can be sure He is never going to change the way He feels about me.

He is good and He is kind, and He is merciful, and He will always be that way.

And He always makes the first move on us.

When He had created the world He stood back, looked at what He had made, and declared it was good, *very* good. (Genesis 1:31 NKJV)

He felt good in His heart about what He saw. The spontaneous goodness and joy of God is behind all, through all and underneath all He is and does.

The cause of His goodness is in Himself.

Just as He *is* love, He does not love as we do, so His very essence is goodness itself, pure, unadulterated, unprocessed, holy, and approachable - goodness.

His goodness is the ground of our faith, our expectation, and our adherence -

*"My soul, wait thou only upon God; for my expectation is from him."* (Psalm 62:5 KJV)

He is good.

And He cannot be any other way.

We will have no ease of heart or soul, no real rest or peace, whilst we seek happiness in things or people, the trivial and the worldly.

We will have no rest because He Himself is our rest, He planned it that way.

You can seek satisfaction anywhere and everywhere and come back to the fact that we were created **by** Him and **for** Him.

We are made in His image.

We will spend eternity with Him.

And we will find our rest in nothing less than He Himself; nothing less than the **nature** of God towards us. And it is His desire that that very nature be formed in us. That we become unchangeable in *our* consistency, constancy, and nature.

It is the pleasure of His good will that He should be our *'all sufficiency'* – nothing lacking – He is enough.

He's enough.

Julian of Norwich put it this way –

*"God **of your goodness**, give me Yourself, for **you are sufficient** for me."*[1]

When you think about it, to ask anything less would not be worthy of Him.

Moses put it this way –

*"Then Moses said, "I pray You, show me Your glory!" And He said, "I Myself will make all My goodness pass before you, and will proclaim the name of the LORD before you; and I will be gracious to whom I will be gracious, and will show compassion on whom I will show compassion.""* (Exodus 33:18-19 NASB)

Moses, backed into a corner by God, cries out for what God most wants to give him – a glimpse of His glory – "*I will make all My goodness pass before you";* and then He speaks of His goodness, His grace, and His compassion; His nature.

El Shaddai, the All-Mighty God, the breasted One, the Nurturer and Sustainer of all things created, speaks of His eternal goodness and all sufficiency to that which He has made.

Latterly a great saint, Charles Wesley, would put it this way[2] -

> *"O God, my hope, my heavenly rest,*
> *My all of happiness below.*
> *Grant my importunate request*
> *To me, to me, Thy goodness show.*
> *Thy beatific face display*
> *The brightness of eternal day.*
> *Before my faith's enlightened eyes,*
> *Make all Thy gracious goodness pass;*
> *Thy goodness is the sight I prize*
> *O might I see Thy smiling face:*
> *Thy nature in my soul proclaim,*
> *Reveal Thy love, Thy glorious name."*

The **glory** of God is the **goodness** of God; God is GOOD.

He is kind-hearted, gracious, good natured and benevolent in intention. He never has a bad thought about anybody and all the things He is, He is perfectly, infinitely, and eternally.

44

He always has been, and He always will be – exactly like this.

I joyously declare to you that the glory of God is the goodness of God.

That He is immutable in His goodness towards you.

He never, ever, changes the way He feels towards you.

What He was, He is and always will be and He calls **you** into an intimate relationship with Himself.

That you might *know* Him.

Really know Him.

Mind that gap.

[1] Julian of Norwich, 'Revelations of Divine Love' Penguin Classics 1982 p 68
[2] 'The Knowledge of the Holy' page 85 Harper San Francisco, 1978.

# 11

# When He is pleased

God is enthusiastic – excited, eager, passionate, fervent, keen, wholehearted - about *you*, who you are and who you are becoming, and He wants you to have a right view of Him in order that you may partner together with Him in these days in all that He has for you.

*"He is present in continuous and perpetual eagerness, with all the fervour of rapturous love, pressing His holy designs."* [1]

He's wooing you beloved...this is a love affair...

And, when that time comes, He is going to be as pleased to have you in heaven as you are to be there – never lose sight of eternity beloved of God; never lose sight of eternity...

When we are pleased, He is pleased.

He is pleased when as His child, you are surrendered to Him; when your will is His will, and His will is yours; He is ecstatic when you trust Him, when you are not in revolt against Him; not seeking your own way; when you trust Him and walk with Him, when you stop resisting Him...

He is pleased.

He is not pleased when you are miserable and unhappy, disconsolate and in despair; when you are out of agreement with Him, but His displeasure is not anger, but compassion at your foolishness. For He would give you all of Himself – it's your inheritance beloved, **He**, is your inheritance and you are His.

I wrote this after a time of meditation -

*Uncreated*
*Shoreless Ocean*
*Awe-inspiring,*
*And Divine*
*Hast Thou said that I*
*May own Thee –*
*Mine?*
*Mine - to treasure*
*Mine - to love*
*Mine - to long for 'til*
*Heaven above*
*Joins us for eternity –*
*In love.*
*Mine,*
*Yes mine, He is mine –*
*Yet, more sublime*
*I am His -*
*And shall be now*
*Forever -*
*Until the earth no longer spins*
*And all of heaven welcomes in*
*Then -*
*He and I in that bright glory*
*One deep joy shall share -*
*Mine -*
*To be forever with Him*
*His –*
*That I am there…*

He is going to be as pleased to have you in heaven, as you are to be there.

Let us lift our voices and praise Him for our creation, salvation and sanctification, for His infinite goodness towards the children of men.

He is eternally and infinitely - GOOD.

Let us put away all doubt and unbelief and trust Him.

Let's hear from Julian of Norwich again -

*"God is all that is good as I see it and Himself is the goodness of all things. All mighty, all wise, all loving, God is everything that is good."*[2]

Simply trusting that is all...trusting in His eternal, immutable, infinite, goodness – His nature - towards us.

Let's pray together shall we?

*Father of glory,*

*You have been pleased thus to reveal Yourself to us, and so we must declare You -* **Good.**

*Assist us to search out as treasure more precious than rubies or fine gold, the infinite beauty of Your nature.*

*With the Apostle Paul, we pray that we may 'progressively become more deeply and intimately acquainted with You' - for we must think rightly about You.*

*Prepare our hearts for eternity; for with You shall we dwell when the stars of night are no more and the heavens have vanished away and only You remain...In Jesus Name. Amen.*

*'Glad Thine attributes confess,*
*Glorious all and numberless.'*
*Charles Wesley*

Selah.

[1] 'The Attributes of God' Volume 1 A W Tozer pp 44 – 45 Christian
Publications Inc. 2003
[2] Julian of Norwich, 'Revelations of Divine Love' Penguin Classics
1982 p 68

# 12

# A new song

Anything that is written or spoken should always point you to Jesus, not to the speaker or writer.

Once I get started on the subject of God, I'm done for.

The truth is, that for me, He is everything I prize, my treasure; everything I hold most dear and precious.

He is life's summum bonum - that's Latin for *'the highest and chief good'*.

He has been that to me since the day we met in 1984 - me at my wits end - Him just waiting for me to come to the end of myself so He could step in and rescue me -

*"He brought me up out of a horrible pit,*
*Out of the miry clay,*
*And set my feet upon a rock,*
*And established my steps.*
*He has put a new song in my mouth—*
*Praise to our God;"* (Psalm 40: 2 - 3 NKJV)

My life has been transformed by Him.

*"In Him I live and move and have my being..."* (Acts 17:28 paraphrase)

I had never really loved anyone before we met.

50

He totally captivated my heart.

I fell head over heels in love.

He ruined me for anything else.

So when I get on my favourite subject, I dive deep into Him; can't stop talking about Him as the old song goes.

I ask: what else is there that is of **eternal** consequence other than knowing **Him** as He really, really is?

A knowledge of the Holy -

*"This is what the Lord says:*

*"Let not the wise boast of their wisdom*
*or the strong boast of their strength*
*or the rich boast of their riches,*
*but let the one who boasts boast about this:*
*that they have the understanding to know me,*
*that I am the Lord, who exercises kindness,*
*justice and righteousness on earth,*
*for in these I delight,"*
*declares the Lord.""* (Jeremiah 9:23-24 NIV)

This short stay car park that is our life here, is but a preparation for eternity with the One who loves **us** with all His heart, soul, mind, and strength - the way He asks us to love Him.

He never asks anything of us except He first gives to us, so He gives us His love, to love Him with, how cool is that?

*"We love because He first loved us."* (1 John 4:19 NIV)
I find it incredible that the Creator of the universe should set His love upon us.

Have you ever taken time out to think about that?

The One who put the very universe together, who put you together, and holds everything together by the power of His Word, looks upon and sets His love upon fallen man.

Awesome.

Breathtaking.

If we are to be of any significance in this time, we must stop our rush and hurry and take time to contemplate and develop a knowledge of Him; the Holy One; a knowledge of the Eternal One.

If you hadn't discovered this already nothing in the Spirit comes on top of rush and hurry.

God isn't caught up in our busyness.

There really are no casual friends in the Kingdom.

God isn't under pressure.

He's not biting His nails there wondering how to put right the next mess the world gets itself into.

He lives in a relaxed atmosphere of rest, love, joy, and peace.

Wouldn't you appreciate some of that?

It's His desire for you.

But there are no short cuts beloved.
You are going to have to carve out some quality time and spend it with Him, until *He* is satisfied that you are beginning to know and experience Him in His fullness.

Government health warning on this one though - it's addictive.

The more time you spend with Him the more you want.

He puts a hunger in your heart - a hunger and thirst - just like it said in the Beatitudes, for righteousness.

How about it beloved, how about it?

You only get one shot at this - why not make it count…

For eternity.

# 13

# The Divine Conquest

There was an old song, a line of which goes - *'A man chases a girl (until she catches him)'*. Composer, Irving Berlin.

It is totally the opposite with God.

He chases us until He catches us and then we say, *"I found the Lord".*

His pursuit of us is relentless.

He will not rest Himself until, having captivated you, He captivates your heart.

Two different things here.

You can make a mental assent and come into the kingdom, but then there is the little matter of your heart.

Your affections.

He's **jealous** for those.

For your **unshared** love.

Your **unshared** devotion.

When that is in the right place, everything else aligns itself underneath.

But while your affections are set on something other than Him, you are like a dog's hind leg - just pause here please and look at your dog's hind leg or anyone else's dog for that matter - you will see it's bent.

The point I am making is that we are *born* out of alignment with Him, and we don't come straight back in automatically the moment we are born-again.

It takes years sometimes to get us to get go of the things we think we can't live without and find that actually **He** is the only One we cannot live without.

So, how's it working out for you?

Just how much of your heart and life *has* He got?

Try drawing a pie chart marking out what things are filling your heart; you may be in for a surprise at how little He has.

Inconvenient enlightenment coming up - He won't rest Himself until He has your whole heart and life beloved, all of it.

Your *unshared* love and affection.

That'll be it.

He is a jealous God.

*"I am jealous for your love, for your talents, and your time"* [1]

We could be hitting some white water shortly so make sure you are fastened in your little craft securely.

We're going to touch some sore spots in the next couple of days, but it's all good; we need to get some things out of the way.

And I must get back to my script, which is looking at what God sees as the *normal* Christian life - His resurrection life and power working through you.

---

[1] Ruth Fazal, *"I am a jealous God"* track 7, "Who is this?" Volume 2.

# 14

## What hinders you?

That's a good question for a start, *"What hinders you?"*

We need a road sign here, 'bumps ahead'.

What hinders you from giving Him your unshared love?

*All* your time and *all* your affections?

What hinders you from living in resurrection life and power?

Maybe you have never thought about it before.

You *'made a decision', 'gave your heart to Jesus'*, a long time ago and then you went to church and that was it; until you get to heaven.

Normal service resumed.

Boring.

Monotonous.

Nothing changes…

Life goes on.

You really don't have the joy you hear people talk about.

You can't 'feel' Him or experience His love.

Others do and it just makes you feel sad, and rather isolated; perhaps even angry.

Beloved, perhaps no one has ever really explained what happened the moment you believed.

What happened sweetheart was you got a 'new for old' policy come to fruition.

It paid out.

You got the goods.

You know, the house insurance policy that gives you new for old if anything happens to the old.

Well, something happened to your 'old' the moment you believed - in fact it happened way before you were born. Jesus took your old life on the Cross at Calvary over 2,000 years ago and crucified it with Himself, and in exchange He gave you a completely new life and a new start.

*"I know"* I can hear you say.

Beloved, allow me to correct you - you ***don't*** know, that's the problem or your life would show it.

Your new start, your new DNA, is still in the packaging, waiting to be unwrapped.

Sitting on the sideboard, untouched.

Do you know that your old life cannot hurt or influence you unless you allow it?

Unless you let it; unless you *empower* it by living there and constantly talking to it?

So, question: are you conversing with a corpse?

Are you ministering in a graveyard?

Your new life can't benefit you unless you *empower* it by choosing to live there.

Present past or present future?

So, which is it going to be?

The new or the old?

No brainer.

But I leave you to think about it because you may have never thought about it before and that package on the sideboard is glinting in the sunlight just begging to be opened…

# 15

# Being cruel to be kind

In a lovely little book by Max Lucardo *'You are Special'*[1] he tells the story of a little wooden person, Punchinello, who was covered with spots and marks that other people put on him. He didn't realise that the stickers he carried only stuck if he let them, until he met Lucia who had no stickers, and he went to visit Eli, the carpenter who, he discovered, made him. Eli told him who he really was, and his stickers began to fall off.

Delightful little tale.

So, we take up where we left off yesterday.

Your old life and all its pain, rejection, hurts and memories, can only hurt you if you continue to *let* it.

The stickers only stick if you let them.

If you *allow* them to.

You now have a choice - old or new.

Tough call I know.

New life or live in the cemetery of the old; difficult choice that.

But this is what happened the moment you believed.

Jesus lifted you out of all that trash; washed you in His own blood; gave you a new heart; a new DNA and a new beginning; that's what is in the box on the sideboard that you keep eyeing and not opening.

So, like I said yesterday, what hinders you?

Before you tell me, *feelings* have nothing to do with this.

Your will has everything to do with this, mixed with faith.

Life in the Spirit beloved, is about the will.

If you are *willing*, you can come to Him right here, right now on your own and tell Him about everything that has hurt, wounded, or defiled you, let go of it, and He will heal you and take the power of those memories away. But you must be willing to let it all go and ask Him to heal you. Just think of it this way it isn't your 'stuff' anyway, it's His, He paid for it all on Calvary's cross, so you need to hand the lot over, don't you? It's not yours to keep.

Another thing, willing – willing not to take pleasure any more in going over how badly you were treated. Some people do beloved, hard as it may seem, they do, relish going back, feeling justified in behaving the way they do in anger, rage, and bitterness of spirit, because of what happened to them 70 years ago.

They keep this wooden chest in the attic of their lives and from time to time, when they really want to *enjoy* feeling miserable, they go up there and start taking things out piece by piece, rehearsing, the hurts, wounds, resentments, bitterness; everything that is attached to the memories. They magnify it all and derive comfort from it; but in doing so, sure enough, it all gets bigger until their past is not only their present, but their future also.

What a waste of a life.

A bit more inconvenient enlightenment is required.

Everything negative that isn't removed from your life, the enemy will *attach* himself to like a leech, sucking the lifeblood out.

Now there's a thought.

You could be ministering death to yourself consistently.

If this describes you, you could be giving legal rights to the enemy too, to torment and distress you simply because you are living from the wrong place.

I'll let the scripture put it plainly for you -

*"One with Christ in Glory*

*Christ's resurrection is your resurrection too. This is why we are to yearn for all that is above, for that's where Christ sits enthroned at the place of all power, honour, and authority! Yes, feast on all the treasures of the heavenly realm and fill your thoughts with heavenly realities, and not with the distractions of the natural realm.*

*Your crucifixion with Christ has severed the tie to this life, and now your true life is hidden away in God in Christ. And as Christ himself is seen for who he really is, who you really are will also be revealed, for you are now one with him in his glory!"* (Colossians 3:1-4)

So, as I said yesterday – what's holding you?

---

[1] Max Lucardo, 'You are Special' Crossway Books, Wheaton, Illinois.

# 16

# Freedom

When Jesus died for us on the Cross, He did not die just to enable you to believe and go to heaven when you die, He died so that you could be set free from the bondage of yourself now in this life.

That could be a revelation to some right there.

He died not just that you might have the freedom of forgiveness of sin but from **yourself**.

That negative, critical, judgemental, anxious, fearful, petulant, fretful, Adamic self.

The self that is full of anxiety, dread, negativity, fear, and panic.

He died so that you might experience **full** redemption of your body, soul, and spirit.

So that you could enjoy partnering with Him as you learn what it means to be a new creation in the Christ.

That is what He means when He talks about being a new creation, He means, be free in the true sense of the word. That is why He never speaks to the old person, but to the new. To who you are becoming, not who you were.

He's never present past with you, He's always present future, because that is all He sees; you in the future.

It is also why you often don't understand what He is saying because you are hearing with your old ears and seeing with your old eyes, and you don't recognise yourself when He speaks.

You can only perceive and know His plan for you when you cross over the line into the territory that is yours, your land of promises in Him, and begin to take the ground.

It is called life in the Spirit.

And it is always about territory.

Specifically, *your* inner territory.

It you are still living in your soul - your mind and emotions - you will be constantly pulled down; constantly tossed around; circumstances will govern whether you are happy or not because everything depends upon what happens; up and down, all the time, no real peace, rest, or stability.

If, however, you are beginning to dip your toe in the water of Life, you find that life in the Spirit is all about your ***will***, not about your feelings; it's about your choices.

Major track change here for some.

Cause of stumbling for others.

You know pleasure is physical; happiness depends on what happens; and joy is a choice.

This is why, I keep talking about you making choices - good ones, right ones.

Because what you *choose* really will determine your destiny.

Your choices will also determine your mental and physical health, beloved.

As attitudes determine altitude, choices determine destiny.

God has a destiny and a purpose for you far above that which you could ask or think, but He's not meeting you on the ground of your soul - on what you 'feel' - He meets you where He always has met you, in your spirit.

God is *Spirit*.

If you are unaccustomed to living life from the innermost part of your being, your spirit man, allow me to introduce you to a new place from which to live, the place where you are in Christ, who is in the Father, which makes you insulated twice over from what is happening around you. Your spirit, the innermost part of you; from here you can live *above* your circumstances - because that is where He has placed you - have a look at Ephesians sometime if you don't believe me.

Life in the spirit is about **displacement**.

And we start with redeeming our thinking **Romans 12:1,2.**

We have another thought; not one that Satan put there, but *another* thought to displace that negative one.

Get a grip!

We are about to have some *'instead of'* moments - we'll look at those tomorrow.

Stick with the programme it's only difficult - if you allow it to be so.

# 17

# Instead of

When Jesus stood up in the synagogue in the Gospel of Luke and all eyes were fastened upon Him, He declared His mandate and He spoke about the radical change that would come by the **Spirit** with the proclamation of the Gospel -

*"The Spirit of the Sovereign Lord is on me,*
*because the Lord has anointed me*
*to proclaim good news to the poor.*
*He has sent me to bind up the brokenhearted,*
*to proclaim freedom for the captives*
*and release from darkness for the prisoners,*
*to proclaim the year of the Lord's favour and the day of*
*vengeance of our God,*
*to comfort all who mourn,*
*and provide for those who grieve in Zion—*
*to bestow on them a crown of beauty*
***instead of** ashes,*
*the oil of joy*
***instead of** mourning,*
*and a garment of praise*
***instead of** a spirit of despair.*
*They will be called oaks of righteousness,*
*a planting of the Lord*
*for the display of his splendour."* (Isaiah 61:1-3 NIV)

He starts here by telling us how this will come - by the **Spirit** of the Lord.

As I said yesterday, nothing radical is going to happen unless it comes from the Holy Spirit to your **spirit**.

It *will* make its way into your understanding in due time, but first it is your spirit, your human spirit, that is impacted by God and the way He started, is the way He goes on.

Paul says -

*"Brothers and sisters, when I was with you I found it impossible to speak to you as those who are spiritually mature people, for you are still dominated by the mind-set of the flesh. And because you are immature infants in Christ, I had to nurse you and feed you with "milk," not with the solid food of more advanced teachings, because you weren't ready for it. In fact, you are still not ready to be fed solid food, for you are living your lives dominated by the mind-set of the flesh. Ask yourselves: Is there jealousy among you? Do you compare yourselves with others? Do you quarrel like children and end up taking sides? If so, this proves that you are living your lives centred on yourselves, dominated by the mind-set of the flesh, and behaving like unbelievers. For when you divide yourselves up in groups—a "Paul group" and an "Apollos group"—you're acting like people without the Spirit's influence."* (1 Corinthians 3:1-4)

He enables us to see just exactly what it looks like if we are dominated by a fleshly, natural, 'feelings-oriented' mind-set - we behave and think like unbelievers…we are subject to the same divisions, strife, arguments, anger, jealousies, fears, and disappointments - the list goes on and on.

But, led by the Spirit of God, things are completely different -

*"But the fruit produced by the Holy Spirit within you is divine love in all its varied expressions: joy that overflows, peace that subdues, patience that endures, kindness in action, a life full of*

*virtue, faith that prevails, gentleness of heart, and strength of spirit."* (Galatians 5:22-23)

Lovely I hear you say, I'll have some of those.

They are yours for the choosing beloved, for the choosing.

In our Christian walk it is always the same, we do what we can, and God does the supernatural.

But unless we do our part, He cannot do His.

God cannot if man will not.

We are meant to be renewed in the spirit of our **MIND** and that will mean ongoing choices as Paul tells us in -

*"Stop imitating the ideals and opinions of the culture around you, but be inwardly transformed by the Holy Spirit through a total reformation of how you think. This will empower you to discern God's will as you live a beautiful life, satisfying and perfect in his eyes."* (Romans 12:2)

That will do for a start; stop imitating the ideals and opinions of the culture around you.

Two-word counsel - stop it!

Instead - be renewed in your thinking.

Over to you.

# 18

## You be you

I asked God – *"What is it You want to be through me?"*

Immediately the answer came back -

*"Myself"*.

Well…He would, wouldn't He?

Years ago, He kept saying to me, *"You be you and I will be Me and that will be enough"*.

Sometimes I think I have the comprehension and attention span of a gnat!

I just forget.

It's the human condition - the enemy still snatches away the seed.

Have you experienced that?

How he snatches the word God spoke to you away and you are left scratching your head?

What He is saying to me He is saying to you also - whatever your situation or circumstance, be at peace -

*"I will be Myself through you and everything will be all right"*.
Paul said it this way-

*"I have been crucified with Christ; it is no longer I who live, but Christ lives in me; and the life which I now live in the flesh I live by faith of the Son of God, who loved me and gave Himself for me."* (Galatians 2:20 NIV)

No longer two lives to be lived, but one, His through you.

This is the normal Christian life.

His life flowing unhindered through you.

Effortless, effective, amazing.

But it's the letting go bit, isn't it?

We find it so hard to let go and just let Him be Himself through us.

Nevertheless, sounds good to me.

I'm up for letting Him be everything in me and through me.

You know the old saying - He can't do through you what He hasn't been able to do in you.

Just imagine what your family, your workplace, your neighbourhood, would look like if you really let everything go to God and let Him be Himself through you.

Yahoo!

*"These who have turned the world upside down have come here too."* (Acts 17:6 NKJV)
That'll be it.

The normal Christian life, turning the world upside down.

Again, I ask, what hinders you?

# 19

# We have lost something

Those early disciples had something we have most definitely lost.

They were **radically** transformed when they heard the Gospel.

It poses the question - what have we done with the Gospel?

Have we just made it an invitation to a slightly higher lifestyle with a promise of heaven on the side?

The ones who turned the world upside down thought nothing of dying for what they believed. Indeed, it is said that some lasted two weeks on the cross singing, praising God and encouraging one another before they died…

They were so convinced in the deepest part of their being that Jesus was God and that He had come to forgive, redeem, rescue, and transform them, that their lives and those around them were turned utterly upside down.

Would you die for what you believe?

When we meet someone radical like that these days, we are apt to say, they are *'too extreme'*; *'too single minded'*; and *'they will get over it'*; and of course, it certainly isn't for us, we're British – dammit!

But beloved, it is.

For us that is.

It is the *normal* Christian life.

We are meant to be head over heels in love with Him and excited about Him and what He is doing every single day.

We are meant to be amazed; to marvel; and to be full of wonder...

At this point if you are suspecting that your Christian life is something other than how it should be, or you would like it to be, can I respectfully suggest you go back to the Master, kneel before Him, and ask if you can start all over again, seeing things the way *He* sees them? Ask Him to give you a spirit of wisdom and revelation in the knowledge of *Him*.

As an aside, you might also give Him permission to be the Author and Finisher of your faith and take your own sticky hands off the building process.

That would probably result in progress immediately.

Give it a whirl.

See how it works out for you.

And, oh, do let me know, I would be really interested to hear.

# 20

# The key to your heart

For more years than I care to remember I have thought that most problems with Christians having a right view of God have been caused by doubt and unbelief.

But as I have meditated on Romans 12:2 NKJV, I am coming round to the view that it could be more about the way they *think*, than downright unbelief.

Furthermore, I think that the key to their heart is their head. It is in the way they think and perceive.

Consider this for a moment - if you have a wrong view of God, based on your early years and your experience of your own father, who was less than perfect, you have without realising it, formed a mindset about what God is like.

Unfortunately, that mindset is completely at variance with the truth of Who He is, and Jesus told us that the truth would set us free.

Father has declared that He wants us to know Him -

*I want you to know Me,*
*Know My holiness*
*Know My perfection*
*Know My joy*
*Know My love*
*Know My goodness*

*Know My plans*
*Know Me*
*Know Me*
*I want you to know*

*Me...*

*And I have given you My Holy Spirit for this express purpose that you might know Me; become more and more intimately acquainted with Me...*

Some of you are in a stuck place.

And you need to take God up on His offer to know Him as He really, really is.

To help you in the process, may I suggest you take two sheets of paper? On the first the heading will be: *'How I see God'* on the second *'What the Bible tells me about Him'*.

Using your sheet headed *'How I see God'* list how you see Him. Be real, don't put what you think you should put, be real.

Then take a slow, thoughtful, look at **1 Corinthians 13**, which shows you a little of what the love of God looks like, and **Galatians 5:22-23**, that reveals the fruit of His Spirit; both describe something of the ***nature*** of God.

What He is really like.

Now, take the second sheet of paper headed *'What the Bible tells me about Him'* and list what you found in the two scriptures you have just looked at.

When you have done the exercise, do a comparison; you can see your current mindset versus who God really is and a little of what He is really, really like.

As a result of your findings, do you need to change your mind?

If you do, throw that first sheet away – preferably burn it - and concentrate your thoughts on the second.

Be **transformed** by the renewing of your mind.

You may discover the key to opening the door of your heart.

I do hope so.

# 21

# The heart

Yesterday I challenged your thinking by asking *"what if the key to your heart was in your head"*; and the key to releasing you from the stuck place you were in, had to do with your mindset.

Specifically, your mindset about God as Father.

And we explored the possibility by doing a short exercise.

I left you to have a mindset replacement, because you can only replace a mindset with a mindset.

Today we are essentially still on the same subject, blockages, hindrances to your intimacy with God as Father.

I am about to share one of the keys I discovered whilst in the healing ministry - your heart, as well as your body, has memory.

It isn't only your mind that keeps a record of what has happened to you.

When the heart has a negative memory carved inside, usually from a painful experience in childhood, it will govern how you see things and people, and most importantly, your view of the Father.

You will see *everything* in distortion.

Proverbs 23:7 NKJV tells us that *"as a man thinks in his **heart**, that is how he will be"*, and I sense we aren't done yet with those of you who find there is a wall between you and God, when it comes to getting close to Him and experiencing Him and believing His passionate love for you.

Today I want you to take a look inside that heart of yours, to see if there are thoughts about God that are not worthy of Him.

Thoughts based on what has happened to you.

Thoughts based on your **perception** of Who He is, not on who He really is.

If you had a distant father, there physically but not emotionally for you; if he was harsh, authoritarian and critical; maybe you could never come up to the standard he held out; perhaps he ignored you; or didn't have time for you, work always had to come first and there was just no time left for you; you didn't feel accepted by him, let alone loved or approved; all these things and more will be imprinted on your heart, and you will still be carrying them…

Beloved, your heart needs a spring clean.

And to do this you are going to have to slow down, find a place where you can be still, talk to Him and listen to what He has to say to you.

You will need to be receptive to what He shows you and be willing to respond.

You will need to be prepared to let go.

You will need to be prepared to change and develop as He guides you.

Most importantly, you will need to remember that the One who knows you best, loves you best…

There is nothing to be afraid of.

Everything to gain, nothing to lose.

So, if you are still in that stuck place, and really desire to get out, take time out to do business with Him.

He is longing for an intimate relationship with you; where as a much-loved child, will you bounce up to Him, jump on His lap and whisper all your secrets into His ear.

Just like that dad you never had…Abba, Father.

He is waiting beloved, and He will continue to wait, outside the door of your heart because the handle is on your side.

Off you go then.

Keep in mind the chief end of man is to glorify God and enjoy Him forever.

So be sure to *enjoy* Him.

# 22

# Enjoying the challenge

As you grow in God you will find that the challenges don't get easier; you need to learn to embrace and enjoy them, together with the changes they will inevitably bring. As by His Spirit God is able to occupy more and more space inside us, so He steps up the pace of the challenges we face to get all the rubbish out of the way.

We have talked about replacing a mindset with a mindset and have seen that the mind set on the flesh, the earthly, carnal, natural mind, is at variance - more than that, it is at war - with God who is Spirit, and it is we who must move our feet. In all of this, our co-operation is key. He wants us to work *with* Him as He goes about the transformation process.

The Holy Spirit, is absolutely committed to transforming us into the image of Jesus, and the way He does so, is by challenging our current thinking, in order to replace it with His.

In this way, we develop the mind of Christ.

We have said it before, He didn't come to make you healthy, wealthy, and wise, but to transform you, and it doesn't happen all at once.

He's got you, now He sets about transforming how you think, perceive and live - now He is after your heart.

He bought you back from the slave-market of sin and He is teaching you how to walk free and live in a totally different Kingdom, with totally different values.

Like the potter throwing the lump of clay on the wheel, He begins to shape and mould us; He leans intently over the wheel; lovingly applying a little pressure here; nipping off a little there; pulling; lifting; drawing; shaping until at last He is satisfied and a beautiful vessel is formed.

You were created to be the object of God's love; to be the vessel that contains His love...But He can't do through you, what He hasn't been able to do in you.

It is quite remarkable how many of us fight this process, preferring to stay in the bondage of the kingdom of darkness rather than emerge into the light of the new day and the new dawn He holds out to us.

If your current thinking has got you where you are and you don't like that place, the sensible thing is to have another thought; a better one.

That is what is meant by -

*"Stop imitating the ideals and opinions of the culture around you, but be inwardly transformed by the Holy Spirit through a total reformation of how you think. This will empower you to discern God's will as you live a beautiful life, satisfying and perfect in his eyes."* (Romans 12:2)

Pay attention to what is rising in your heart as you hear or read this message.

Is it hope that things could be different - maybe even the glimmer of joy at the thought of a different way of perceiving, believing, living? If it is, that is a pointer to your current mindset being out of alignment with God. You simply need to be willing to unlearn what you thought you knew and understood about Him and His desires for you and your destiny, and replace that with another, better, thought.

Embrace the challenge, don't run from it.

Let your heart go to another place.

As you learn something more about Him, the new thought will expand your heart towards Him.

He wants you to think about Him without fear, confusion, or condemnation; without running, hiding, and shifting blame. He isn't the author of those things; He wants your heart to melt when you think about His goodness, kindness, and unfailing love.

We saw this didn't we when we made our two lists...

You did do that exercise didn't you?

You didn't...?

O.K. I'll just wait here until you do.

# 23
# A legacy

What God had in mind when He created man was an eternal companion for His Son; someone upon whom He could set His love and who would love Him in return, so they might live happily ever after.

He had marriage in mind.

As this person would need to be compatible with Him, He made him in His own image and likeness.

With meticulous care He crafted the being out of clay and when He was satisfied, breathed into it His own life; and it became the very first living soul.

Calling the Federal head of the human race Adam, God placed him in the Garden He had already prepared and gave him a command - just one - which would in the event, prove to be his downfall, as it was a test of his trust in the veracity of his Creator. The command was this -

*"You can eat from any tree in the garden, except from the Tree-of-Knowledge-of-Good-and-Evil. Don't eat from it. The moment you eat from that tree, you're dead."* (Genesis 2:17 The Message)

Simple enough.

You can eat everything but -

*THAT.*

Thus warned, when Eve came along and the first marriage took place, Adam told her God's one prohibition, *"not that tree dear."*

It all worked very well, until Satan threw a grenade into the middle of the garden one lovely morning, which revealed a fatal flaw in the heart of Adam.

Given free will, despite the perfection that surrounded them both, when push came to shove, he was as open as his wife to questioning the Almighty's motives towards them, when the serpent sidled up and whispered -

*"Did God really say?"* (Genesis 3:1 NIV)

*That* beloved, is your legacy from the Federal head of the human race, Adam.

Suspicion about God, and His motives.

Can He *really* be trusted?

When you chose to believe in Jesus, you were raised to a higher place than Adam.

A heavenly place.

The one place where you could get all your prayers answered and all your needs met; the Father placed you *in* His beloved Son, Jesus.

*Now* you can trust and believe that God is good and has nothing but good plans for you.

*Now* His eternal love pours out on you in the same way as it pours out on Jesus; you live under His smile; He declares He is pleased with you, even though you haven't done anything to earn His pleasure; He loves you with the same intensity as He loves His only Son. When He looks at you, He sees nothing wrong with you, He sees you complete, in His Son.

But you still have that question – *"Did God really say?"* (Genesis 3:1 NIV) constantly posed by the enemy of your soul.

*"Did He **really** say, He loves **you** in the same way as He loves His Son?"*

The implication being *"He can't possibly, look at you, just who do you think you are?"*

No wonder God says in -

*"Now, if anyone is enfolded into Christ, he has become an entirely new creation. All that is related to the old order has vanished. Behold, everything is fresh and new."* (2 Corinthians 5:17)

Brings a new slant to it doesn't it when you lay the old alongside the new.

You can clearly see why the old must go.

God had to deal with it. Nothing was worth salvaging. A new start was required. All of it, with its legacy of distortion and lies; unworthiness; blame; shame; running, hiding and fear, and so now you are no longer *in Adam*, but *in Christ* -

Let's just look at the old for a moment -

*"When I heard the sound of You coming in the garden, I was afraid because I am naked. So I hid from You."* (Genesis 3:10 The Voice)

You don't want to live there, naked, afraid; running and hiding; shaming and blaming.

Time to come out of agreement with *that* wouldn't you say?

I thought you would.

Let's do this thing then – let's say it together -

*"I am a new creation in Christ, the old has gone, the new has come. Amen".*

Now all we need is to *believe* it…

Mix it with FAITH.

# 24

# The Potter's wheel

You were created for God to love you.

He needed an object upon which to bestow the fulness of His love, so He made you.

If that didn't come clear in the last message, I hope it will now.

He **sets** His love on you because He has an eternal purpose in creation, and you are part of that purpose.

There's more of course.

Keep in mind the Potter's wheel.

Whilst He loves you without condition, He isn't about to leave you where He found you, that's why you are on the wheel; there is a little work to be done to prepare you for eternity with Him, as His Bride.

Sometimes, we lose sight of the fact that He has an eternal plan and while he is working and forming the clay that is us, He sees the culmination of that plan -and He is perfectly satisfied - you are just what He was looking for.

For some of us, this is probably the biggest stumbling block.

We don't *feel 'worthy'* of His love.

We *feel* the need to do something to earn it.

So, we try every which way to make ourselves '*feel*' more acceptable to Him.

Let's settle this, none of us are worthy and we cannot earn His affection; He loves us because He loves us, because He loves us!

His choice.

Plus, nothing.

And He made us for Himself.

*Creation* was *His* idea; *salvation* was *His* idea; our reigning and ruling with Him for eternity was *His* idea; it has nothing to do with our worth or lack of it; it has **everything** to do with **Him**...

And the value that He places on what He created, which is you, is unlimited.

It is so simple we want it to be more complicated.

He plans for eternity, and you are part of that plan.

Go back to the beginning Genesis, Adam, Eve, wedding.

Go to the end, Revelation, Jesus, Bride, wedding.

He didn't redeem us and go to all that trouble just so we could to heaven, live a life of bliss for eternity, see all our relatives and friends and so on; all this is in order that He has a Bride for His Son, a people fit to reign and rule with Him for eternity.

Because God **plans** for eternity.

Another gap, I think.

# 25

# 1 John 4:19

*"We love, because He first loved us."* (1 John 4:19 NIV)

We love Him because He loved us first…

**That's** first love.

His, for you.

Not yours for Him.

And unless you have **received** His love, there is no way you can love Him.

You *cannot* love God with your human, natural, love.

It takes God to love God.
Human love is fallen, it is a travesty of the real thing.

It seeks only that which is best for it.

It is self-centred.

Track everything back, even your love for your child and your spouse, and you will find it is all about **you**, how it affects, *you*.

Hard pill, but there it is, swallow it.

We are all about *"what's in it for me"*.

It is self-referential.

Everything about us is.

It's a result of the Fall.

Goes through us like a stick of Blackpool rock.

We can't help it; but we are not meant to stay like this.

We can learn a different way of loving if we are willing to ask Him to transform us to love as He loves.

So we see everything and everyone through His eyes of love and acceptance.

By His transforming power we can become those vessels of honour, receiving, and carrying the love of God -

*"For it is Christ's love that fuels our passion and motivates us, because we are absolutely convinced that he has given his life for all of us."* (2 Corinthians 5:14)

Paul speaks from **experience**, not book learning.

Paul knew all about the latter, but Jesus captured his heart, and it turned the Pharisee upside down and inside out. He ends up saying *"for me to live is Christ, to die is gain"*. (Philippians 1:21 NIV) - he was a ruined man for anything other than Jesus.

We are nothing and can do nothing unless He has captured us and captivated our hearts…and transformed our love and everything else about us into *His* likeness.

Something else to turn your thinking upside down - He loves you because He **chose** to love you; He **set** His love on you; we receive that love and pass it on - that's the only time we are of any real use here on earth; when we receive *His* love and give it away.

When you leave first love, you have left the love *He* has for you and gone into trying to perform, to work for His approval, earn it - or something equally obnoxious to Him -

The church at Ephesus:

*"I know all that you've done for me—you have worked hard and persevered...But I have this against you: you have abandoned the passionate love you had for me at the beginning. Think about how far you have fallen! Repent and do the works of love you did at first."* (Revelation 2:2,4)

What were their first works of love?

Simply loving *Him* passionately with the love He poured out on them. Thereby they were putting the first commandment firmly where it belonged, first; *"love the Lord your God with all your heart, soul, mind and strength"*, and then go out and love your neighbour as yourself.

They had tried doing it the other way around, as have we, and ended up out of alignment with Him, which attracted His loving correction.

We have so much to learn about what love really, really, is when God speaks of it - it will take eternity to get our hearts and heads around it.

We can only glimpse what He is saying.

Our problem comes when we can't or won't, for whatever reason, receive what He freely desires to give us, His *unshared* love, which is what He asks of us in return.

Our unshared love.

How's yours?

# 26

# Loving the God who loves you

Like so many words in our vocabulary, the word 'love' has lost its true meaning, that is if it ever had one, other than the current sexual connotations that are attached to it.

There are several types of love in the Greek language, **storge** - nurture love - the love of a mother for her child; the love of friendship - **phileo**; sexual love – **Eros** - never used in the Bible; and finally **Agape**, the self-giving love; the love of *choice*, the love that took Jesus to the cross.

'Phileo' and 'Agape' are beautifully illustrated in the dialogue between Peter and Jesus at the point when Jesus restores Peter after his denial -

*"**Jesus**: Simon, son of John, do you love Me more than these other things?*
*__Simon Peter__: Yes, Lord. You know that I love You.*
*__Jesus__: Take care of My lambs.*
*Jesus asked him a second time ...*
*__Jesus__: Simon, son of John, do you love Me?*
*__Simon Peter__: Yes, Lord. You must surely know that I love You.*
*__Jesus__: Shepherd My sheep. (for the third time) Simon, son of John, do you love Me?*
*Peter was hurt because He asked him the same question a third time, "Do you love Me?" Simon Peter: Lord, You know everything! You know that I love You."* (John 21:15-17 The Voice)

'Love' is used throughout this dialogue, but they were using different terms and Peter was missing Jesus. Peter was using the friendship word for love, *'Lord, You know I think you are a great guy; you know I phileo you.'*

Jesus on the other hand was using - Agape - the love of choice that lays down its life. The self-giving love that asks nothing in return, but continues to love no matter what comes back, be it good, bad, or ugly. So, Jesus asks the question of Peter -

*'Simon, son of John, do you agape Me more than these other things?'*

*'Do you love Me in the way in which you choose to give up everything else, even your life, to put Me first, to follow Me, and do as I am asking you?'*

He then proceeds to tell Peter how he will end his days...

*"I tell you the truth: when you were younger, you would dress yourself and go wherever you pleased; but when you grow old, you will stretch out your hands, and someone else will dress you and take you to a place you do not want to go. Jesus said all this to indicate the kind of death by which Peter would glorify God. After this conversation, Jesus said,*

*Jesus: "Follow Me!"* (John 21:17–19 The Voice)

Sooner or later if you mean business with God, He will come to you with the question -

*"Do you love this more than you love me?"*

As He transforms us and conforms us to the image of Himself, our love is transformed, and we no longer seek to possess that which we say we love.

Did you know that our natural love seeks to acquire, and having acquired, to possess and finally control that which it says it loves?

Natural love, what we understand as love; the one we talk about all the time is, I must inconveniently enlighten you is **Eros**. The self-centred, self-consuming love, that seeks *possession* of that which it loves.

If you don't believe me, get before God and ask Him to show you, preferably from your own life.

Ooops, mind the gap.

# 27

# The battle for the soul

What all this shows us, is that though we're born again and safely on our way to eternal bliss, the battle hasn't ended, in fact it has intensified.

Now we fight it on two fronts.

The natural and the spiritual. Now you are in the Kingdom of light, the enemy of your soul doesn't just stand there wringing his hands in despair, giving up.

You have moved kingdoms from the kingdom of darkness into the Kingdom of light and in doing so, you have become a threat to him. You are stronger than you think, more powerful than you realise and more beautiful than you can imagine, and he has lost control over you.

What a defeat!

Undeterred though, day and night he seeks to find a chink in your armour where he can gain entry and where he can find a reason to accuse you before the Throne of Grace. Now he intensifies his efforts to malign you before the Father - accusing you day and night – e.g. John 13:2, Ephesians 4:27, 6:11, Hebrews 2:14, Revelation 12:10.

He never wins of course because Jesus steps up in the Divine Court of Heaven and says – *"That one is mine I paid for them Father"* and Father in turn declares *"Case dismissed".*

But on the ground, where we are, we can find this battle strenuous and exhausting, unless we know exactly where we stand, and who we are *'in the Christ'*; it is so brilliant we must read the whole scripture -

*God's Power Raised Us from the Dead*

*"And his fullness fills you, even though you were once like corpses, dead in your sins and offences. It wasn't that long ago that you lived in the religion, customs, and values of this world, obeying the dark ruler of the earthly realm who fills the atmosphere with his authority, and works diligently in the hearts of those who are disobedient to the truth of God. The corruption that was in us from birth was expressed through the deeds and desires of our self-life. We lived by whatever natural cravings and thoughts our minds dictated, living as rebellious children subject to God's wrath like everyone else.*

*But God still loved us with such great love. He is so rich in compassion and mercy. Even when we were dead and doomed in our many sins, he united us into the very life of Christ and saved us by his wonderful grace! He raised us up with Christ the exalted One, and we ascended with him into the glorious perfection and authority of the heavenly realm, **for we are now co-seated as one with Christ!**"* (Emphasis mine). (Ephesians 2:2-6)

Spiritually we are now seated far above Adam, our Federal head, and originator of the race.

Adam was placed on the earth, **we** are placed in Christ, and with Him, the risen, exalted and glorified One, in heavenly places; we are **in** Him as He is in the Father, and we are loved by the Father as He loves His Son –

*"Don't you believe that the Father is living in me and that I am living in the Father?"* (John 14:10)

94

As this becomes a reality to us, we see that we fight *from* victory, not towards it; that we do have a choice now, where we live our lives from and whom we serve.

This is the whole of our battle from the moment of our salvation - choosing to live in the Kingdom of light with its completely different value system. Choosing to say a resounding *"No"* to Satan and self, and an equally resounding *"Yes"* to God.

It isn't easy, but something as glorious as this isn't going to be easy, is it?

The Kingdom of God, as we have seen, is upside down.

Mind that gap.

# 28

# Living in two realities

For some of you my talking about the two realities of the heavenly and the earthly may be completely new and somewhat foreign at first.

The introduction of a new truth always causes disruption to us.

When it first comes, the truth is almost always received negatively.

It upsets our fruit basket and then some.

Right now, we are being unsettled from our place of comfort, into looking at a different dimension; maybe one we have never realised existed, or one that we have preferred to ignore.

The truth is beloved of God, we live in **two** realities.

Our feet physically here on the earth.

Our spirits, seated in heavenly places, in Christ.

Our journey is to come to the realisation that the heavenly, though we cannot see it, is the superior of the two, the more real of the two; and is where we *must* live from, as spiritual beings.

Earthbound as we are, affected by situations and circumstances that surround us, we are apt to say, *"that's too heavenly minded to be of any earthly good",* the reverse is the truth; unless we see things from a heavenly perspective, we are doomed to lose the battle with the adversary every single time, because we are fighting on his level; on the ground of his choosing.

God the Father has placed us high **above** all this, in order that we may reinforce His Son's victory on the cross and defeat the enemy while we are here on earth. We are a law enforcement agency on the earth. We can seek the strategy of God for any and every situation or circumstance.

We call it prayer.

We find out what plan God has to defeat our current situation or circumstance, ask, and see it happen.

If not sooner, then later.

Remember Daniel - it took the angel sent to answer his prayer 21 days to reach him and bring him succour - so great was the battle in the unseen realm.

The heavenly battle is real and immediate.

Jesus overcame *all* the powers of the evil one on the Cross - and so can we, in Him, but it is a process, a process that takes a lifetime.

Life in the Spirit is about two things: displacement and choices.

We will have to displace our current understandings and mindsets and continually choose the higher path, as He shows us.

We will need to be this for the long haul not the short sprint.

We will need to become constant, not tossed to and fro.

We will need to be steadfast and immoveable always *"abounding in the work of the Lord..."* (1 Corinthians 15:58 NIV)

We will need to set aside earthly claims and focus on the heavenly.

But that is where we started this session - it is the *normal* Christian life, it's just that we haven't seen it up until now.

A life as Jesus described it – of abiding in the Vine.

How about it beloved?

How about it?

The choice is yours.

Turkey or eagle, you get to choose.

# 29

# Turkey or eagle

I began "Mind the Gap' by saying *"everything has been converging on this point".*

We had looked at the Sermon on the Mount and what Jesus says is our pattern for living, our paradigm. We saw we cannot possibly live the life He described without the empowering of the indwelling Holy Spirit.

We discovered we had some basic misunderstandings, which we looked at last time, setting ourselves the right way up. And we were now going to look at the *normal* Christian life as envisaged by Jesus; the glory of the Cross; living in resurrection life and our *experience* of God.

I finished yesterday's message with this phrase the life of *"abiding in the Vine".* The reason being we are no longer growing from the old stock, the old vine, of our fallen Adamic nature, but we are in vital, living, union with the True Vine; now we no longer occupy one territory but two, so we live in two realities; we are both earthly and heavenly beings.

We fight on two fronts: we are subduing our earthly, lower nature and bringing it under the benevolent dictatorship of the Holy Spirit; and we are law enforcement officers; enforcing Jesus's victory over the enemy of our soul -

*"But the one who indulges in a sinful life is of the devil, because the devil has been sinning from the beginning. The reason the*

*Son of God was revealed was to undo and destroy the works of the devil."* (1 John 3:8)

I left you asking if you wanted to be a turkey or an eagle.

It's pretty obvious what I mean; turkeys grub about on the earth, eagles fly high…

At the start of the session, I suggested maybe you would have some decisions to make - decisions that will determine your destiny; adopting attitudes that will determine your altitude, whether you want to be a turkey or an eagle?

Know this, He isn't going to love you any the less whatever you choose.

The choice is entirely yours.

By choosing to be an eagle you will come into everything Jesus won for you on the Cross - it all depends on just how much of Him you really want…30, 60, 100%.

Should you choose 100%, you will experience a life of resting in Him; heaven on earth and an eternal perspective on life -

*"As we enter into God's faith-rest life we cease from our own works, just as God celebrates his finished works and rests in them."* (Hebrews 4:10)

It's the choice of doing things your way, or His way.

By the Spirit, or by the flesh.

Neither way is without difficulty and sometimes pain.
And there are no short cuts.

Oh boy. Let me outta here!

You can go round and round in the wilderness like the children of Israel for 40 years, or you can decide to be an eagle and find yourself soaring to heights you could never have imagined.

Not much of a choice I know(!), but it's yours for the taking.

If you decide to be an eagle life will begin to have certain disciplines attached.

You will find you need to set aside quality time to be with the Father, when you would probably prefer to be doing something else. Your friends and family may begin to think you have developed another head, and in a way, you have - a spiritual One - you are now under new management.

Submitted to the benevolent dictatorship of Another.

His name is Jesus.

You will also find that you develop an eternal perspective, seeing everything in that light…the things of the earth will grow strangely dim…

How about it?

Remember, you only get one shot at this thing.

# 30

## Sitting on the fence

I suspect many reading this will be doing just that.

Sitting on the fence.

You are looking at everything that is being said and understanding it, but you are reluctant to plunge in and experience it, because you do not know what that would mean.

You are sitting on the fence.

You are worried about what you might have to give up or lose.

Inconvenient enlightenment coming up – when the opportunity of a lifetime presents itself, you must act within the lifetime of that opportunity. You may lose the opportunity to make the choice if you procrastinate.

*"Reach out and touch the Lord as He passes by…"*[1]

Beloved, there is nothing that you will be asked to surrender that hasn't been **given** to you in the first place. He is the Source of all things - David recognised this in his prayer of dedication of the Temple -

*"Everything comes from you, and we have given you only what comes from your hand"* (1 Chronicles 29:14 NIV)

*"We have given you only what comes from Your hand"*

Comes the time when we must recognise that He is the source of everything; everything comes from His hand; who we are, what we say we own; our families, *everything*, comes from one source and one only - Him.

The Creator, Sustainer, and Upholder of the universe.

We came into the world with nothing, and we leave the same way, and while we are here, we steward everything and own nothing.

When we own it, we seek to possess and control it.

**Mine.**

We reach for it, grasp it, and hold it.

When we open our hand, when we release everything back to the One who gave it, He in turn gives back good measure, pressed down, running over into our laps.

But first - we need to let go.

That is why some of you are fence sitting right now.

You are not even counting the cost; you are just sitting there - observing.

Because it is all about letting go.

Ah, letting go.

There's the rub.

The fact is, unless you *"taste and see that the Lord is good"*, Psalm 34:8 NIV; unless you experience Him for yourself, you will remain on that fence thinking about it, until it is too late.

Sooner or later, like the Israelites - what a lovely object lesson they are - something will need to jerk you out of your reverie.

Isaiah had it right when he said to them -

*"Lift up your eyes on high,*
*And see who has created these things,*
*Who brings out their host by number;*
*He calls them all by name,*
*By the greatness of His might*
*And the strength of His power;*
*Not one is missing." (*Isaiah 40:26 NKJV)

The gaze of the people had dropped; their thoughts of God and His majesty had gone; they looked only on useless idols; they were in darkness and decline. They looked to the nations around them for help and found none. They worshipped idols who could not speak.

They had left first love.

The One who loved them and brought them out of Egypt, into a land of plenty.

It is *so* easy for us to be the same.

If we persist in living from the old stock, Adam.

We get into a rut.

You know what that is - definition of a rut – it's an open-ended grave.

Quiet time; daily reading; prayer list; something to be got over so you can get on with the day.

Sooner or later, we find we are starved; we no longer sense Him, hear from Him, or expect to; we know we don't really communicate with Him and now we are nervous to try.

We no longer stretch ourselves, or take risks in God; instead, we look for safety doing just as those around us; captive to the culture, we walk in suspicion; fearing the same things as they do so we store up for the future 'in case' some disaster should strike -

*"Now, off you go! I am sending you out even though you feel as vulnerable as lambs going into a pack of wolves. You won't need to take anything with you—trust in God alone. And don't get distracted from my purpose by anyone you might meet along the way."* (Luke 10:3-4)

And they left all and followed Him.

It's the **normal** Christian life, beloved, the *normal* Christian life.

[1] Mission Praise England, No 193, Bill Harmon, copyright 1958 Gospel Publishing House.

# 31

# Ever increasing faith

There is a little book by Smith Wigglesworth with this title - ever increasing faith. There is so much truth in the phrase because we should be going from faith to faith.

From one degree faith to another.

Going higher, travelling with God, increasing in confidence in Him, growing in grace every day.

Is that your experience?

Or have you somehow got stuck along the way?

Have you forgotten that this is *His* eternal plan worked out in His way, unfolding for your life?

Perhaps you are not availing yourself of the grace, the endless ocean of grace, which is there for you every single day as you travel.

God's actions towards you are based on who He is; not on who you currently are not; not your performance, or perceived lack of it, as a believer.

Sometimes that is all we need to remember.

God is *not* performance driven.

He isn't results driven either.

If He was, Jesus failed dismally, only twelve were left, and they all ran away.

Need to get this thing the right way up again.

Everything comes down from the Father of Lights in whom there is no shadow of turning.

There's no darkness where He is.

He makes no shadow.

He is Light, pure light.

*"This is the life-giving message we heard him share and it's still ringing in our ears. We now repeat his words to you: God is pure light. You will never find even a trace of darkness in him."* (1 John 1:5)

Everything starts with Him and ends with Him.

He is the Author and Finisher of our faith, the Alpha, and the Omega.

He initiates, we respond.

No longer two lives to be lived, but one.

His through you.

He isn't performance driven.

We love because He first loved us.

And rest.

Ah, rest.

That would be the rest of faith -

*"As we enter into God's faith-rest life we cease from our own works, just as God celebrates his finished works and rests in them."* (Hebrews 4:10)

Have you seen the whip in the hand of the enemy of your soul - he's always telling you 'you haven't *done* enough'; 'you're not *good* enough'; 'you need to *do more* to be acceptable'.

Begs the question - how much is enough?

It's all lies.

Join the **grace**-awakening beloved.

*"So here's what I've learned through it all: I eave all your cares and anxieties at the feet of the Lord, and measureless grace will strengthen you."* (Psalm 55:22)

It's **all** grace.

*"And since it is by God's grace, it can't be a matter of their good works; otherwise, it wouldn't be a gift of grace, but earned by human effort."* (Romans 11:6)

That'll be it.

**AMAZING –**

**GRACE.**

# 32

# Grace

A prominent Old Testament word describing God's grace is 'chesed', dropping the 'c' we pronounce it 'hesed'. The word speaks of deliverance from enemies, affliction, or adversity. It also indicates enablement, guidance, forgiveness, and preservation.

Grace is the indwelling Presence of God delivering us from the evil one, keeping us, preserving us, and bringing about a permanent change within us - back to the Lord's prayer again.

'Thy Kingdom come *in* me' we are saying when we recite it.

Grace starts where we end.

When we have come to the end of trying to apply paint and wallpaper; change ourselves by our own efforts; pull ourselves up by our bootstraps; we find that the only way was, is and always will be, grace.

Not a work of our hands, but totally His.

Grace means God moved heaven and earth to save those who could not lift a finger to save themselves; grace is God sending His only Son to the cross so that we the guilty ones might go free, be reconciled to Him, changed into His likeness, and received into heaven when the time comes.

Grace comes down to us to change us into beings fit to live in heaven with Him for eternity.

Grace is God's *love in action* towards us.

It's amazing as the hymn says.

And He has oceans of the stuff.

Sometimes though, because of the way we are brought up, we enter Christianity thinking that either we *can* do all this ourselves, or we *have* to do this by ourselves as we have been taught.

It is then we find that everything God asks of us, He gives us.

We cannot love unless He loves through us.

We cannot be kind unless Ho is kind through us.

We cannot keep going unless His steadfastness keeps us.

We cannot be patient, long-suffering, peaceful, or gentle, unless it comes from Him. On and on it goes, and eventually we find that the only way to do this thing is the rest of faith by grace.

*"By grace are you saved through faith"* (Ephesians 2:8–9 NIV) the way you come in is the way you go on -

*"Throughout the coming ages we will be the visible display of the infinite, limitless riches of his grace and kindness, which was showered upon us in Jesus Christ. For it was only through this wonderful grace that we believed in him. Nothing we did could ever earn this salvation, for it was the gracious gift from God that brought us to Christ!"* (Ephesians 2:7-8)

Sort of settles it really doesn't it.

Even our initial, saving faith, came from Him.

All our struggling and striving, blood sweat and tears avail us nothing.

Zilch.

We can do nothing but *receive* His grace.

Receive.

Now there's another problem.

We do have a problem receiving, don't we?

There's a solution though - ask Him to help you to receive everything of Himself He really wants to give you.

It's *all* Him from first to last.

Problem solved.

# Section 2

## 'His Majesty'

*'The Chief end of man is to glorify God and enjoy Him forever.'*

Westminster Shorter Catechism

# He will glorify Me

We are in a time where God is uncovering absolutely everything.

He is peeking underneath those fig leaves with which we have covered ourselves, and without warning it seems, is ripping them off.

Everything we have used to cover ourselves to escape from His scrutiny is being exposed.

Exposed.

We don't like that.

Some of us would much prefer to live in darkness than light, but there it is.

We have cried out for revival; for visitation; for Presence; for Him to come down.

And now He has; and in His mind, is habitation, not visitation.

He's come to dwell, stay, and remain in us and with us.

This means that things we have held on to, like ways of protecting ourselves; defending ourselves; coping; all the mechanisms that exclude Him; beliefs we have cherished which commence *"I like to think…"* are being thrown out.

And just like over 2,000 years ago when Jesus walked the earth, it wasn't as they expected, liked, or wanted a lot of the time; He particularly upset the religious crowd, it's just the same for us.

Times they are a'changin.

God has come down to **inhabit** His church not just visit it.

And we are blinking at the light and feeling the heat and for some, the pressure.

This process will not stop until Jesus comes, because the Holy Spirit has come to speak of Him; and the fire of His presence within us, is burning up all the dross -

*"But when He the Spirit of truth comes He will guide you into all truth, for He will not speak on His own but will speak only what He hears and He will tell you things yet to come He will glorify me for He will receive what is mine and tell it to you."* (John 16:13-14 MOUNCE)

That is a literal translation from the Greek because I want you to see clearly, this is all about His revelation of Himself.

That is the purpose of the Holy Spirit within you - to speak of Jesus, and glorify **Him**, there has been a shift from what you want, to what He wants.

No longer will what you know, or like to think about Him, hold any security for you because He is after your heart, He's making no apologies, and He's coming after you with romantic intent to reveal Himself in His Majesty.

*"Bring it on"*, we say, until we discover what that means.

In His parlance, that does not mean a warm fuzzy.

Habitation is not driven by what you want, but by what He wants and what you *need*.

His *government* in your life.

Whoops.

The change of management that took place the moment you were born again…you have an on-high calling now, and a new direction for your life

You can seek for healing and deliverance, and it is right that you do, but primarily these are there to lead you to *Him*, that you might **know** Him.

He is corralling His church.

He's got her in a corner, just as He did with Moses when he cried out *"I beseech Thee show me Thy glory".* (Exodus 33:18 KJV)

That wasn't Mo's idea beloved, God backed him into a corner and put that desire in his heart and then He said, *"O.K. then, I will let all my glory pass by you, but I will hide you first; and it is only safe, incidentally, for you to see My back."* (Paraphrase Exodus 33:20 KJV)

Why only His back?

Crisp time folks.

If Moses saw the glory of the Lord full on, it would have been more than having a close-up view of the sun.

God revealed a little of Himself to Moses who saw - *His Majesty.*

He is bringing the word Majesty back into our vocabulary.

He is setting His Bride on her feet, making her beautiful, preparing her in *His* way, for *His* coming because her wedding is very near.

Get used to the word *'passion'* - His for you and yours for Him.

And get used to the word *Majesty* because that is Who He is.

### His Majesty.

This session is going to upset everyone at one time or another; I predict than none of you will like everything, or even some things, but they need to be said.

That said, if you have your hardhat; asbestos suit; and sunglasses; fasten your seatbelt, we are, once more, cleared for take-off.

# 2

# Martin Luther

Have you ever heard this quote from Martin Luther? For me it is priceless because I know he is describing me absolutely and I revel in what he describes:

*"Now is this not a happy business? Christ, the rich, noble and holy bridegroom, takes in marriage this poor, contemptible and sinful little prostitute, takes away all of her evil, and bestows all His goodness upon her! It is no longer possible for sin to overwhelm her, for she is now found in Christ and is swallowed up by Him so that she possesses a rich righteousness in her bridegroom."* [1]

Isn't that the absolute truth of the matter, it is no longer possible for sin to overwhelm us because we are *in Christ* and swallowed up by Him, and He has bestowed all His goodness on us.

Wow! What about that!

I do hope that is a reality for you, because without it you are still poor.

All your treasure comes from your position *in* the Beloved.

Paul says *"In me dwells no good thing".*

It's a death blow to our ego to find that in us dwells nothing worth keeping; that everything **must** be made new because paint and wallpaper wouldn't cut it; but it is the key to our liberation too - that God placed us where we could have everything we need to grow into the likeness of His Son, in place of the likeness we had before in Adam…

We must be assured of this, or we will limp along trying to make ourselves better; trying to improve the old; and fail dismally all the time.

That's why God the Father placed us *in Him* the moment we believed.

He put us in the one place where we can get all our needs met and all our prayers answered.

*"Oh,"* I hear you say, *"He doesn't answer mine…"*

That is because beloved; you have slipped out of where He put you.

You aren't *abiding* in the Vine.

You aren't dwelling, remaining, staying, where you were put.

You have stepped away from being under the shelter of the Most High (psalm 91). And like the church at Ephesus, you have left your first love; you've walked away.

So, you see the problem what you perceive as the answer; and you pray and you might as well have left things alone because your prayers hit the ceiling.

The problem is you aren't in line with what Jesus and the Holy Spirit are praying.

You haven't brought yourself under the benevolent dictatorship of the Holy Spirit, stayed where Father put you, and so you have prayed according to your own understanding, not in alignment with His will and purpose for your life and specifically, your current situation.

Be of good cheer, it is easily remedied - take a look at this -

*"This is the [remarkable degree of] confidence which we [as believers are entitled to] have before Him: that if we ask anything according to His will, [that is, consistent with His plan and purpose] He hears us."* (1 John 5:14 AMP)

This is the key to getting prayer answered every single time.

We come before Him.

Ask Him what He wants to do in the situation.

Ask Him to do it.

See the result.

Never fails.

He has told us it will always work so we have a *"remarkable degree of confidence".*

It's brilliant!

And He loves it, the connection He gets with you, and the fellowship that ensues as you spend time with Him, discovering His best for your situation.

Never fails.

Try it and see.

You won't be disappointed - guaranteed.

[1] www.thegospelcoalitiion.org quoted by Alister E McGrath in Christian Spirituality, An Introduction (Oxford 1999) pp158-159

# 3

# Have you got it?

So, our being exposed is one thing; Who He is, is another; His gaze is penetrating our belief systems right now, and He must have a very good reason for doing so.

What His gaze has fallen upon is just what we believe about Jesus and who He is; what salvation, sanctification and justification mean; and He says -

*"Have you got it?"*

That seems a strange question to ask at this stage, when we have travelled so far together, but Jesus asked the same question of the disciples after they had seen many miracles and travelled with Him for some while.

He wanted to know who they said He was exactly -

*"Who do you say I am?"* (Matthew 16:15 NIV)

This question followed the miracle of the loaves and fishes and a confrontation with the Pharisees who were asking for a sign…so they had seen the supernatural provision.

It also followed His statement that their eyes seemed to be sightless; their ears, unable to hear -

*"Knowing what they were thinking, Jesus said to them, "Why all this fussing over forgetting to bring bread? Do you still not see*

*or understand what I say to you? Are your hearts still hard? You have good eyes, yet you still don't see, and you have good ears, yet you still don't hear, neither do you remember. When I multiplied the bread to feed more than five thousand people, how many baskets full of leftovers did you gather afterward?"* (Matthew 16:17-21)

*"Twelve," they replied.*

*"And when I multiplied food to feed over four thousand, how many large baskets full of leftovers did you gather afterwards?"*

*"Seven," they replied.*

*"Then how is it that you still don't get it?"*

He asks us the same question -

*'How is it you still don't get it?'*

And He suggests to the disciples that their hearts are still hard.

A hard heart is an unbelieving heart - a heart that sees and hears all the things Jesus has done, but still *cannot* believe, *cannot* trust, insists it doesn't understand.

So He asks them another question - *"who do **you** say that I am?"*

Interestingly He doesn't say who do you believe I am, but what does your mouth say I am; what comes out of your heart about Me and Who I am to you? He links both.

Saying and believing -

*"When Jesus came to Caesarea Philippi, he asked his disciples this question: "What are the people saying about me, the Son of Man? Who do they believe I am?"* (Matthew 16:13-15)

They answered, "Some are convinced you are John the Baptiser, others say you are Elijah reincarnated, or Jeremiah, or one of the prophets."

"But *you*—who do you say that I am?" Jesus asked."

He presses the question.

And asks His closest followers who they think He is.

First of all, they tell Him what others are saying about Him; it is Peter who has had the revelation, he says -

*"You are the Christ, the Son of God".*

Jesus says then -

*"Jesus replied, "Blessed are you, Simon son of Jonah, for this was not revealed to you by flesh and blood, but by my Father in heaven.""* (Matthew 16:17 NIV)

The revelation of who Jesus really is comes to Peter from the Father.

It comes to each of us the same way.

So, question, who do *you* say Jesus is?

The question is more important than you may think as I will explain tomorrow, but for today do you have a personal revelation of the fact that Jesus is God and He is the Promised Messiah, and you are now in Him seated in heavenly places?

If your faith is on a solid foundation, you have nothing to worry about, so I'll let you think about your answer and we'll continue the discussion tomorrow.

# Personal revelation

I was talking yesterday about having a *personal* revelation that Jesus is the Christ, the Anointed One, the Promised Coming One; the One, foreshadowed right the way through from Genesis to His first appearance in the Gospel of Matthew and shown in everything that the Jewish nation enjoyed In their tabernacle and temple worship.

I say first appearance, because of course, He is coming again soon; *"Soon, in your understanding of the word"* as He said to me recently.

It may have seemed a very strange question to leave you with after the length of time we have been travelling together, because I took it for granted that you know Him; know exactly who He is -

His Majesty, the King.

All the colours, the drapes, the furnishings and accoutrements in the Old Testament had a message about the One who was to come - they were 'types' or 'shadows' of His Majesty.

It's a brilliant study on its own; but my purpose in asking this of you is because we have to get something straight - just who do *you* think, believe and say Jesus is?

Not what He can do for you, but Who He is?

If you do not have this firmly in your heart, that He is the Christ, the Son of God; God incarnate, made manifest; the sinless, spotless Lamb of God; your whole theology will have an unstable foundation and you will spend a lot of your time wobbling and be an absolute push-over for the enemy.

If Jesus was just a prophet, a good man, but not God incarnate, your salvation could be seriously in question because if Jesus isn't God, but just some sort of an amazing man, He came from the stock of Adam and His blood will not cleanse you, nor will it save you. One thing rather leads on to another you see, and the Virgin Birth is very, very, important.

And the fact that He is God.

He is the I AM.

The Self-Existent One, who was and is and always will be; take a look at **Luke 10:18** sometime, it shows He was present before creation…

He came to earth and was born of a virgin.

That is true by the way.

He was born of a virgin.

That means the blood flowing through Jesus' veins did not carry the Fall and all its consequences. It carried Eternal Life and that Life saved us from our sin and justified us - made us right with God - when we believed in Him.

These are things we must settle at the front end.

Jesus Christ is God, and His blood is spotless and *eternally* efficacious to cleanse, heal and deliver us.

The reason I raise these issues is because someone told me recently that (largely) in their denomination they did not believe Jesus to be God. He was a good man and a prophet, certainly, but not God.

Ooops!

That explains why so much else is completely on the tilt; why it feels more like a club when I visit with them, than the company of the redeemed.

Their foundation is out of kilter.

You may want to think about that for a moment, because what I am travelling towards is what your thinking is about, who Jesus is, why you were saved, apart from eternal bliss.

What you *think* about God is the single most important thing in your life.

So, I'll leave you to settle this one in your own mind before we go any further.

# 5

# Majesty

So we're talking about Majesty.

Specifically, *His* Majesty.

The Majesty revealed on the Mount of Transfiguration; at the beginning of the book Hebrews and the Revelation of Jesus Christ, in the book of that name.

I can't resist it -

*"The Son is the dazzling radiance of God's splendour, the exact expression of God's true nature—his mirror image! He holds the universe together and expands it by the mighty power of his spoken word. He accomplished for us the complete cleansing of sins, and then took his seat on the highest throne at the right hand of the majestic One."* (Hebrews 1:3)

Yes!

See what happens at the unveiling of Jesus in all His glory when He appears to His friend John, at the beginning of the book of Revelation. When He appears to tell him what is coming - John, who had known Him in His humanity, is floored by what he sees.
He falls on his face.

Jesus as a Man was O.K.

Different, but O.K.

Jesus as His Majesty…something else again.

Hear how he struggles to express what he sees -

*"When I turned to see the voice that was speaking to me, I saw seven golden lampstands. And walking among the lampstands, I saw someone like a son of man, wearing a full-length robe with a golden sash over his chest. His head and his hair were white like wool—white as glistening snow. And his eyes were like flames of fire! His feet were gleaming like bright metal, as though they were glowing in a fire, and his voice was like the roar of many rushing waters. In his right hand he held seven stars, and out of his mouth was a sharp, double-edged sword. And his face was shining like the brightness of the blinding sun! When I saw him, I fell down at his feet as good as dead, but he laid his right hand on me and I heard his reassuring voice…"* (Revelation 1:1-17)

John adopts the position - face down, as good as dead.

This is *normal* for those who have encountered His Majesty; face down, as dead - you see it in Daniel and Ezekiel, their reaction to His Majesty is to fall on their faces…as good as dead.

This Jesus, the Warrior King, who will shortly return to claim His treasured possession; His bride; you, is Majestic; He is the King of kings, and Lord of lords.

A bit of inconvenient enlightenment there, He isn't coming back as a baby in a manger.

He is coming back as the Warrior King, the Creator and Ruler of all things, to judge the world.

This is your Lover, your Shepherd, and your King.

Your Maker and your Sustainer.

In Him you live and move and have your being. (Acts 17:28 NIV)

Here He is up front and personal, and the only response is awe, wonder, and falling flat...

If at present you only know Him as your Saviour, He will soon be revealing Himself to you as your Lord.

If you have only taken Him as your Saviour, soon He will be asking you *"Will you let Me reign over you?"*

Only you can answer that.

He won't love you any the less.

His love is unchanging

It pours forth day after day, whether it is reciprocated or not.

It's not human love.

It is Divine love.

Agape.

The self-giving love of choice.

The love that goes on giving...

The love that expects nothing in return.

Amazing.

We just glimpsed glory and Majesty.

6

# Saved to serve

The denomination into which I got saved was what I would call 'works' oriented, so I got the strong conviction very quickly that I was *"saved to serve"*. This was all right as far as it went, but in their eyes, it meant I was saved to: do the tea rota; look after the children; give lifts to those who needed them; oversee the bookstall; make cakes as necessary; put the chairs out; put the chairs away, clean the toilets...

Get my drift?

It was only after many years that I discovered that yes, I am saved to serve, but not my church, my denomination - I am saved to serve -

**HIM.**

And He isn't looking for workers, but worshippers.

However, if He asks me to polish the pews; vacuum the floor; dust the silver; light the candles; wash the dishes; clean the toilets; welcome at the door, any of a thousand ways of helping, I will do it – as an act of *worship* and service, to Him no problem.

But unless He is the one asking me, the answer is no - because everything I do, He initiates because I worship and serve **HIM** first, not the church building.

I am here to serve Him *first* - then you.

131

I am here to love Him *first* - then you.

Everything flows out from that love relationship with Him - **first**.

Out of my love relationship with Him, comes my call and my service to - you've guessed it – Him first, then others.

I wonder how differently our churches would run if we *all* asked Him what He wanted us to do rather than putting ourselves on a rota because that was what we were asked to do by the pastor - we might even see the Kingdom come before our very eyes.

Just a thought.

Provocative I know, but there you go.

Out of the comfort zone.

# 7

# What if?

Developing the thought from yesterday a little. Just how much of what we currently understand of 'necessities' in church do we actually need when we meet?

What would happen if we didn't have tea and biscuits after the service - or before it if you are really avant-garde?

What would happen if we didn't have the P.A.

Or the music group.
The screen for the words we sing.

The dance group.

The flag wavers.

The speaker.

The ministry teams.

The creche.

The children's work.

Just questions.

What **could** happen if we just came together with the express purpose of putting **Him** first; with a heart prepared to worship *Him*; to minister to *Him*, alone?

If every person came with a heart to worship and lift Him high.

Could He resist coming down?

The Lord inhabits the praises of His people.

Whilst all these things are useful, perhaps necessary, and I in no way wish to demean them, what could happen if we focussed less on the external and more on our internal condition and heart towards Him?

Less on whether or not the coffee was hot; the notices were too long; and we don't like the music or the way the vicar (or whoever) speaks and anyway he goes on for too long.

What would happen if we realised the word 'service' means *our* priestly service - towards **Him**?

It's about whether He is pleased or not, not us…

Whether *He* feels welcome or not, not us.

Maybe in the places where He isn't welcome and cannot move, the Holy Spirit would come.

I'm not calling Him the Spirit, because He is Holy and a lot of us have completely forgotten that too.

He is Holy, and we are meant to be the same, set apart for the purposes of God.

Sanctified.

That in a sentence is what holy means - set apart for the purposes of God.

Sanctified.

Set apart.

For *His* purposes.

We seem to have lost that along the way somewhere.

It's the restoration of the Creator/creature relationship again, getting this thing the right way up.

We are called 'saints' - why? We are set apart for His purposes - the sanctified ones.

Now there's a thought.

You are set apart, by God for Himself, for a purpose that you may yet not know – is it time to start seeking Him for your God-given purpose do you think?

You have a *purpose* you know…

That'll cure your boredom.

I'll leave you with that one.

# 8

# Other things

As we are talking about things like sanctification; the basics - like what it means to be a saint and set apart for God; what about your understanding of exactly what happened the moment you believed?

A lovely teacher now with the Lord, made a list of 37 things that happened the instant we believe on Jesus and receive Him as our Lord and Saviour.

Now there's a thought, **Lord** and Saviour.

Many people are happy to take Jesus as Saviour, but they stumble when it comes to the Lordship bit.

You might like to consider praying this, I call it 'the Lordship prayer'; like the act of baptism, it changes who governs your life:

*"Lord Jesus, I acknowledge my need of you and I accept you as my Saviour, my Deliverer and my Lord.*

*I invite you now to be the Lord (the authority, and to be in control of, and be the final decision maker) in the whole of my life.)*

*Lord of my human spirit and all my spiritual awareness and worship.*

*Lord of my mind, my attitudes, my thinking, my beliefs and my imagination.*

*Lord of my emotions and my expression of my feelings – anger, grief, joy etc.*

*Lord of my will and all my decisions.*

*Lord of my body, my physical health, my exercise, my diet, my rest and my appearance.*

*Lord of my sexuality and its expression.*

*Lord of my family and all my relationships.*

*Lord of my secular work and my Christian service.*

*Lord of my material goods and my perceived needs.*

*Lord of my finances..*

*Lord of my plans, my ambitions and my future.*

*Lord of the manner and timing of my death.*

*Thank you that Your blood was shed that I might be free from the consequences of sin and that my name is written in the book of life.*

*Amen."*

Sort of takes you a bit further than just being a believer wouldn't you say or a follower?

Into being a disciple?

Maybe?

Totally handing the reins over.

Maybe?

The government of your life…

Maybe?

Letting Him take the lead?

Maybe?

Like joining the army really; under new authority.

That is, if you prayed it from the heart.

# 9

# Included

Included.

We touched on this in an earlier session, the fact that we are 'bone of His bone', in other words; we are part of Him; but that truth rarely becomes a reality for us.

For it to become 'flesh' upon us; that is for it to become a reality and something that governs our lifestyle, needs not more information but revelation.

And that revelation comes gradually, and when God the Father is ready by the Holy Spirit, to impart it to us, just like Peter.

Until then, our part is simply to keep pressing on and into Him, where we have been placed by Divine fiat.

This is where choices become so important.

We have discussed at length that just as choices determine destiny; attitudes determine altitude. If you are choosing to live an earthbound, ordinary, humdrum life; to remain undisturbed, this will not be for you.

If you have a dream to be an eagle and rise to the heights in your Christian walk, this will definitely be for you.

The reason being you are *included* in Jesus.

Included in His death.

Included in His resurrection.

Included in His *enthronement*.

And your fellowship is with the Father and the Son and the Holy Spirit.

So you will understand when Paul says -

*"And if we were co-crucified with the Anointed One, we know that we will also share in the fullness of his life. And we know that since the Anointed One has been raised from the dead to die no more, his resurrection life has vanquished death and its power over him is finished. For by his sacrifice he died to sin's power once and for all, but he now lives continuously for the Father's pleasure. So let it be the same way with you! Since you are now joined with him, you must continually view yourselves as dead and unresponsive to sin's appeal while living daily for God's pleasure in union with Jesus, the Anointed One."* (Romans 6:8-11)

Because this scripture has become flesh on you; it is real. You understand what co-crucifixion means and reckon yourself dead to sin and alive to God - all the time.

Watchman Nee wrote a book about it *'The Normal Christian Life'* - if you read it, you may find it is far from normal, compared with the life you are living right now, but it will certainly give you more than a taste for the 'high' life. Life lived from a different perspective, a different place - enthroned with Jesus, His Majesty.

An amazing thought that – enthroned with Jesus...

Why not spend a few minutes just dwelling on it, we need to learn to slow down.

# 10

# Majesty Divine

This one isn't going to be one for everybody, but for those for whom it will hit the spot it is needful.

*"Shoreless Ocean! Who shall sound Thee?*
*Thine own eternity is round Thee,*
*Majesty Divine."*

That is a stanza of verse by one Frederick William Faber[1], a writer and mystic of the 19th century.

When you really set your heart upon pilgrimage, sooner or later you will find yourself drawn to the mystics. Those people who spent their lives gazing on His Majesty, meditating on Him, and wrote about what they saw.

Most of them had very hard lives, full of pain and deprivation; persecuted by the church of their time; hounded from place to place; but their heart's desire to know Him never wavered; and their legacy remains.

There is a way in which we are becoming more and more superficial in our Christianity; more and more concerned with feelings, than with knowing Him. That isn't a criticism, it is an observation; it is the result of the time and the culture in which we live. But for those whose hearts are not satisfied, who long for more of Him; those in whose hearts there is a cry ascending to Heaven -

*'Is that all there is?'*

Reading and meditating on the thoughts of these ancients will bring a measure of relief. To begin with you will discover you are not alone in your quest. There have always those who have desired more of God.

The result or your search will be that you say less; much less; and think an awful lot more. Your level of worship won't depend on the PA or the music group; it will be internal and constant; a river, silent, still, and deep; you will have begun to touch the heart of God; words can no longer express what is happening on the inside of you; a kind of sweet delight is forming.

You are becoming a priest unto God and like Mary, you sit at His feet in adoring silence, ministering to Him alone -

*'But you are the ones chosen by God, chosen for the high calling of priestly work, chosen to be a holy people.. '* (1 Peter 2:9 The Message)

Priests minister day and night to His Majesty.

We are all called to be priests to God, we are not all called to a life of mysticism; but if we are, the thirst cannot be quenched; the hunger remains; the quest, inevitable; you *must* have more of Him. You cry with the psalmist – *'One thing I ask of the Lord, this is what I seek...'*

*"One thing I have desired of the LORD,*
*That will I seek:*
*That I may dwell in the house of the LORD*
*All the days of my life,*
*To behold the beauty of the LORD,*
*And to inquire in His temple.*
*⁵ For in the time of trouble*
*He shall hide me in His pavilion;*
*In the secret place of His tabernacle*

*He shall hide me;*
*He shall set me high upon a rock."* (Psalm 27:4–5 NKJV)

This word, then, is for those who are hungry; who identify with the cry; to them it will be a ray of hope rising in their hearts that there is more, much more, to be discovered, found, enjoyed, relished, and explored about this great God of ours, His Majesty. Taste and see the scriptures say, and you just did -

*'The race of God's anointed priests*
*Shall never pass away;*
*Before His glorious face they stand,*
*And serve Him night and day.*
*Though reason raves and unbelief*
*Flows on, a mighty flood,*
*There are, and shall be to the end,*
*The hidden priests of God.*

*His chosen souls, their earthly dross,*
*Consumed in sacred fire,*
*To God's own heart their hearts ascend,*
*In flame of deep desire;*
*The incense of their worship fills*
*His Temple's holiest place,*
*Their song with wonder fills the Heavens,*
*The glad new song of Grace."* [2]

That'll be it.

[1] *'The Christian book of Mystical verse'* A W Tozer, Martino Publishing 2010 *'Majesty Divine '* p.7
[2] Ibid. *'The Royal Priesthood'* p 59 Gerhard Tersteegen 1697-1769

# 11

# His love slave

I talked earlier about us being exposed, and I felt when I wrote yesterday's message that was what had happened to me.

*My* heart was being exposed.

I can keep it hidden most of the time, but when I start wanting to write about God, His Majesty and supremacy, what is hidden begins to surface like a fountain bubbling up from somewhere deep inside me.

I have the heart of a worshipper, no credit to me, it is what He called me to be, and what He is fashioning me to be; the thing I love to write and speak about most is Him…

You will never exhaust His Majesty you see.

Everything else comes to an end.

Everything else never really satisfies for long - it's like empty calories…a house of cards.

Spiritually.

He has put in my heart a deep desire to know Him.

Know how He thinks.

Know His heart.

How He sees things.

How He loves…

These are the things that drive me.

When everything is stripped away; all the busyness of life; all the needs of the sheep; feeding, watering, keeping them clean; only He remains…

Every now and again He focusses me.

Brings me back to ground zero.

Back to kneeling at His feet in rapturous wonder.

The eyes of my heart open to Him.

I'm exposing myself again.

But maybe it is needful; there might just be one person out there reading or listening to this who is saying *'I want THAT; I want what she's got; I want to desire You with all my heart, soul, mind and strength'*.

Should that be the case, then this little message will have fulfilled its purpose.

Signing off for today, in His service, I am, yours sincerely, His love slave.

# 12

# Pleasing the Father

It won't surprise you that the last couple of messages came after a time of worship and fellowship with the Father, Son and Holy Spirit after sensing that pull, that irresistible tug, to *'Come away with Me'*.

It happened that circumstances were such that I could do just that.

Take uninterrupted time out with Him alone.

No phone.

No noise.

No nothing.

Just Him.

Have you ever done that?

Spent the morning, or at least an hour or so, just in the Presence?

He loves every connection He has with you.

He doesn't get that pleasure very often though, does He?

When you love someone enough to lay your life down for them, you are going to want to spend time with them without interruption or distraction - just to love on them a little.
You are going to want their undivided attention and their unshared love.

Not unreasonable.

We would be the same if we had paid such a high price.

He has paid a high price, to secure you for Himself, for eternity.

You are not your own, you were bought at a price.

That is reality.

He bought you; purchased with the blood of His Son; from the slave market of sin and set you in a high place.

He put you in the one place where He could look upon you and love you in exactly the same way as He loves Jesus.

He placed you lovingly and carefully, and oh so deliberately, in Jesus.

So He can call you Beloved.

Relate to you because He has declared you righteousness, holy, and precious in His sight.

 A jewel for which He gave a nation -

*"Since you were precious in My sight,*
*You have been honoured,*
*And I have loved you;*
*Therefore I will give men for you,*
*And people for your life."* (Isaiah 43:4 NKJV)

That'll be it.

That'll be you.

Do you have any idea at all just how precious you are to Him?

*"But you are God's chosen treasure—priests who are kings, a spiritual "nation" set apart as God's devoted ones. He called you out of darkness to experience his marvellous light, and now he claims you as his very own."* (1 Peter 2:9)

It was the Father's pleasure to bruise Jesus to restore you to His heart.

Now He **claims** you as His very own treasure.

He would love to spend some time with you.

Can you just stop a moment and let Him have His enjoyment too?

Would now be a good time?

# 13

# What is love?

Sometimes life deals us such difficulties that we cry out 'What's it all about?' don't we?

Things just overwhelm us; we cry out to Father for help; wondering why He doesn't deliver us from what is assalling us and maybe we conclude that He **doesn't** love us...because if He did, He surely would **do** *something* about it; not just stand idly by observing our pain.

This is when knowing His ways, becomes *really* useful, because it keeps you in a place of peace and rest.

When God speaks about love, He doesn't mean human love as we understand it. He means agape; Divine love, the love of choice.

Agape says whether we are good, bad or ugly He has sovereignly chosen to set His love on us. He has covenanted to do so; and part of that love covenant is that He undertakes and indeed promises, never to leave us nor forsake us.

That means whether we feel or hear Him or not, He is there with us and He will work for us in and through the situation.

(I won't quote **Romans 8:28** at this point as I may cause you to stumble since you will want to do me some harm!)

We are really naive if we think loving us means He is going to make our lives trouble free.

In fact, most Christians would say it all kicked off just after they believed; or even just after they got that pan-galactic prophecy.

It seems that trouble is attracted to us like iron filings to a magnet; consider Job -

*"Man is born to trouble as the sparks fly upward."* (Job 5:7 NKJV)

He knew a thing or two.

The fact is, we are being *trained*; we are in preparation, for something much higher and longer lasting than seventy odd years on this planet; so, there is a very good reason why tests and trials come. We are in training. We are in His school; under His hand; undergoing training for reigning with Him for eternity.

Our finite minds can't grasp something that always was and always will be, but we can understand that this life is our training ground; and when you train for something, like an athlete, you put yourself into and under situations and pressures that others don't experience; and you do it willingly because you know *why* you are doing it.

I can guarantee to you that whatever your situation, no matter how dire it appears, He is absolutely aware of it and is working in it, and in you, through it.

He allows in His wisdom what He could easily prevent by His power, could become a cliche, but it is the truth.

He *never* takes His eyes off you; He is working all things together for your ultimate good; He will either deliver you out of the situation or keep you in and through it.

He is faithful.
That is a fundamental truth about the love of God for you.

Not a warm fuzzy, not a lovely feeling, but truth.

He will *never* leave you nor forsake you, but He will allow everything needful for your growth and development to come across your path; you get to choose whether you thank Him in it (not for it); or revile Him because of it - like Job's wife.

God's love is tough love.

It is training you for reigning.

Keep eternity in mind and start thanking Him that you know and are confident in the fact that He who began a good work in you *will* complete it until the day of Jesus Christ (Philippians 1:6 NIV)

All things, not some things, work together for your ultimate good beloved, they really do.

# 14

# Now hear this

This lovely piece was written by someone I don't know, I haven't her name, but she will recognise herself, a follower of Graham Cooke; if you are reading please excuse me using this without your permission, it's just too good to miss and it speaks of someone who only sees difficulties until they see His Majesty -

*"I saw only fences...*
*You opened gates.*
*I said "I can't..."*
*You said, "I know..."*
*I drowned in my smallness -*
*You overwhelmed me with Your bigness.*
*When I couldn't imagine a future,*
*You whispered and kissed and sang Your song to me until I simply had to follow,*
*Until I found myself standing before a door... knocking.*
*And somewhere in the knocking, in the waiting, I began to dream*
*Of a life beyond the door.*
*At some point, in the knocking, while I waited,*
*You stole my fears -*
*And placed hope in my pockets.*
*I stopped crying about endings and began looking for the beginning.*
*Until the door vanished, when I least expected,*
*And I tumbled into a space so wide, so vast, so blue, so... You,*

*Where there are no ceilings, no walls, not even a floor to restrain me...*
*A landscape without limits...*
*Endless plains of hope...*
*Rivers of renewal...*

*Everest's of imagination...*
*Summits still in clouds, begging to be climbed...*
*I am surrounded here by runners, climbers, dreamers -*
*Explorers who live in the question -*
*"What's out there?"*
*Adventurers without maps,*
*Who navigate with compasses set on True North...*
*So I stand still, listening... resting...*
*And You are smiling at my wonder...,*
*Delighting at my discovery of who You really are...*
*And who I really am -*
*Until I gather myself,*
*And begin...to run... and run... and run...*
*And climb and climb and climb...*
*For You are the summit...*
*You are the peak...*
*Living with You in Your 'Secret Place'...*
*The possibilities are limitless...*
*I have found my heart's desire - in You."*

# 15

## Love is a many-layered thing

There was a song by Andy Williams, years ago - *'Love is a many splendoured thing',* but I am discovering that it is a many-layered thing.

What I mean is that God has to work over many years; through good and bad things; to bring us to the point where we discover that He is enough; He is sufficient; He is our heart's desire, as the poem said yesterday -

*'I have found my heart's desire - in You'.*

That is His goal, to bring us to the place where we really know that we belong to Him and all will be well.

There is no getting away from it, He created us to be complete *in Him*; to desire Him; be satisfied - with Him.

*'Our hearts,'* Augustine it is reported said, *'are restless until they find their rest in You.'*

Some five years ago I took a bad fall down a flight of stairs, the result was that I was out of action for nearly a year; during that time, I discovered something.

He really was *all* I needed.

As isolating as that time was, when I look back, I wouldn't have missed it; because it taught me something I would never have learned any other way.

It's that question *"what do You want to be to me now that you couldn't be at any other time?"*

The enforced circumstances, the confinement, are there so He can give you something of Himself you couldn't receive at any other time or in any other way.

He didn't cause the circumstance - life or the enemy did that - but God means it for good and He wants to be something life-transforming for you, in it.

Your part is to find out just what.

It's called heads you win, tails you win.

Nice one that.

I would sit up in bed at night and listen repeatedly to a track on a Ruth Fazal CD of the same name - *'All I need'*.

It was as though I was **compelled** to listen until I really, really got it - He really, really was, all I needed; *all* of Him for *all* of me…

*"You are the summit...*
*You are the peak...*
*Living with You in Your 'Secret Place'...*
*The possibilities are limitless...*
*I have found my heart's desire - in You."*

I just could not listen to anything else, and through it I found He truly was and is, *all* I need.

He had been saying to me for months – *"I am your all sufficiency".*

To which I would reply, *"I know"*.

But I didn't know.

Not until I was brought low.

I was taken back to the time of my conversion, when I told a man friend - whose association I needed to break - that I was complete; when I finally told him, he freaked out; I was saying, *"I no longer need you."*

But there are many layers.

Love is a many-layered thing.

When we truly acknowledge and embrace the fact that we were made for **His** delight and His alone we become like the maiden in the Song of Songs coming up from the wilderness, leaning on the Beloved -

*"Now I know that I am filled with my beloved*
*and all his desires are fulfilled in me."* (Song of Songs 7:10)

Like that maiden we have to come to the end of ourselves and our ideas first, before we can enter that blessed state of knowing that we are filled with Him, and all His desires are found and fulfilled in us.

Makes you think, doesn't it?

Whatever your current circumstance, the question you may need to be asking is *"What of Yourself do You want to give me that I couldn't receive at any other time?"*

The answer might surprise and delight you.

# 16

# I have started

On one of the TV quiz shows the host says, *"I've started so I'll finish"* as he's asking the contestant questions. I've started talking about just how Majesty impacts on us...

He is not a God afar off, but a God who is near.

So near, in fact, He lives in you.

He likes habitation, not visitation.

In the Old Testament He visited His people; His Holy Spirit came upon them for specific purposes; in the New Testament, He indwells His people. That's upfront and personal.

There is no way you can get away from Him.

You can run to the ends of the earth only to find Him saying – *"What are you doing here Elijah?"* (1Kings 19:9 NIV)

His pursuit of you, of us, His Bride, is fuelled by His passion for us.

Passion is not a word we talk about much - being British.

But when it comes to talking about our relationship with Him - He's not red hot about you, He's white-hot...He's passionate.

He will track you down no matter where you are currently hiding.

He will not be satisfied until you **know** how much you are loved, accepted, and favoured.

*"Why is that?"* you may be asking yourself.

Beloved, His acceptance of you, His approval of you, and His favour on you give you security, significance and self-worth and He wants you to know it, really know it, deep inside. Receiving and living in these lovely truths makes you strong, powerful and a very real danger to the forces of darkness.

And what is more, no-one is safe from a blessing when you are around.

That is the way He intended it - that you should represent Him and bring heaven to earth.

That you should know exactly who you are in His sight and revel in that knowledge.

You are loved, blessed, accepted, and highly favoured.

He is biased towards you. Tough on everyone else, but there it is - you get to be the favourite.

Do you know He feels joy and great pleasure in you? His delight is in who you are and who you are becoming under His Holy Spirit's tuition.

The world really is your oyster.

You have all you need for a life of overcoming and victory; it's just that sometimes it doesn't feel like it.

That's because the Holy Spirit is busy reprogramming you, and life can be a little disconcerting at times; not to mention uncomfortable; but keep the end result in view, you are being conformed to His image, His very nature in love, joy, peace, patience, goodness, gentleness, kindness, long-suffering, and self-control…and you are increasingly displaying the fruit of His Spirit -

*"But the fruit produced by the Holy Spirit within you is divine love in all its varied expressions: joy that overflows, peace that subdues, patience that endures, kindness in action, a life full of virtue, faith that prevails, gentleness of heart, and strength of spirit. Never set the law above these qualities, for they are meant to be limitless."* (Galatians 5:22 - 23)

Limitless, that was what our poem was about…limitless possibilities…

Never forget that you are strong, powerful, favoured, accepted and beloved…His passion.

His beautiful Bride.

# 17

# Limitless possibilities

*"Living with You in Your 'Secret Place'...*
*The possibilities are limitless..."*

What would it look like for you to live with these - limitless possibilities?

That you never said *"I can't"* because you are convinced that you can, because He can.

And since there is now only one life to be lived, His through you, you know He will, if you will allow Him.

It could turn your world upside down.

Kill all those negatives in one fell swoop.

Dead.

Imagine life without negatives – bliss.

Let your heart go to another place on that thought.

Only seeing the best, always.

Only hoping for the best, not writing a scenario of the worst, always.

Seeing the treasure in people not the trash, always.

Ah.

There's a big one…

Could be revolutionary.

We may need to explore a little more of His Majesty and His great heart towards us; come into a better understanding of Who He is and what He wants for us, if we are going to pursue this line of thought.

Not just pie in the sky when you die.

Steak on your plate while you wait.

Let's explore the idea together.

It's a place of abiding.

The promise of limitless possibilities comes to us when we stay where we are put and aren't shaken by circumstances and situations.

That's what it means to abide.

To remain, steadfast and immoveable when everything around you is being shaken.

Staying in Christ, not running around like a headless chicken asking the opinion and prayer of all and sundry but hunkering down in the Secret Place with Him – alone – your all sufficiency.

It's a discipline.

*"I know You. You are allowing this to make me press further into You, and I'm going to do just that"* -
*"Go, my people, enter your rooms*
*and shut the doors behind you;"* (Isaiah 26:20 NIV)

That's a bit out of context I know because it's about God's final judgement, but it was the scripture that came to mind.

Go, enter your room, shut the door - another way of saying stay put, abide, remain, dwell, where God has placed you until the storm passes. You have your very own nuclear bunker…inside His heart.

He allows in His wisdom what He *could* easily prevent by His power, that's true but tests are necessary, you don't launch a boat before it has undergone its seaworthiness trials - same with us, every elevation in the Spirit will be tested and contested by the enemy.

It has to be.

It's allowed to be.

Your part is to stand firm.

Just stand.

Not run, hide, or shift blame, but stand.

How's it working out for you?

# 18

# How much more

Looking again at His Majesty and how He doesn't think the way we do, I tripped over 25 references to *'how much more'* in various versions of the bible e.g., Matthew 7:11 NIV, regarding the way God wants to give to us.

How *'much more'* does He want to bestow His goodness upon us.

How *'much more'* does He want to give good gifts to us.

How much more.

God is a Giver.

He is the Giver of all Givers - He gives above and beyond to those who deserved nothing but wrath and judgement…He gave His only Son.

How much more…

There must be a paradigm shift in our thinking when we become Christians.

Julian of Norwich said it this way -

*"Everything that is beneath God, everything that is less than God, is not good enough for us. For this reason, the soul has no rest until it can stand above every created thing. For nothing made can compare with uncreated God. We must fight to*

*possess this truth because our inner man will always want to find security in the things of this world".* [1]

We must *fight* against ourselves to possess this truth because anything less than Him will never satisfy us, no matter what we may think.

[2] *'Lord, of Thy goodness, give me Thyself for anything less would not be worthy of Thee...'* Julian again.

Nothing that is made can compare with the uncreated Magnificence of God.

We must *fight* against our soul's inclination to find security in the things of this world.

We have to do *violence* to ourselves if we are to come into what Jesus won for us on the Cross.

Our value systems need to change, because His are completely 'other than' ours, take a look at this; the world strives for -

Privacy
Material success
Convenience
Comfort

The Kingdom is about:

Openness and authenticity
Sacrifice
Love
Discomfort/inconvenience

Which one are you currently striving after?

God wants you in the latter of course, where your life is open and authentic; where you love as He does and give without counting

164

the cost because you know His resources are limitless and God is a Giver above all things; and you bear any discomfort or inconvenience for His sake. (Amy Carmichael wrote a book about it, the title is 'If', I'll let you find it for yourself...)

It's that word again, limitless.

Can't get our heads around it can we?

The way He thinks and orders things in the world of His heart.

Lord, give me three wounds: the wound of compassion, the wound of contrition, and the wound of seeking after You...

And He plans for eternity -

*"I saw a stately lord, seated in his regal chamber, before him stood a lowly manservant – respectful and waiting to do his lord's will. The servant waited a long time and it was clear that he felt nothing but love for his lord...Oddly he was dressed in clothes that were scanty, and worn almost to rags, filthy with grime and sweat...and then the lord leaned forward and spoke something private to the servant and the servant rushed from the lord's presence as fast as he could run...'*[3]

Jesus stands before the Father, clothed in the filthy, sweaty, rags of Adam's flesh, eager to perform the will of His Father in the redemption of mankind...

He made us to be His alone, and He intends we have no higher allegiance to anything that is less than Himself.

I salute His Majesty.

[1] I promise you a crown, David Hazard, a 40-day journey in the company of Julian of Norwich, p 43, Bethany House Publishers, 1995.

[2] *'Revelations of Divine Love'* Julian of Norwich, Clifton Wolters, p 68, Penguin Classics, 1982.

[3] Ibid page 24

# 19

# Embarrassment

Sometimes, even in the company of the redeemed, we are embarrassed to speak of Him in the way our hearts are inclined, aren't we?

His Presence in us compels us to recognise His transcendence.

But we stifle it because we really don't know how to handle it – the fire that has been kindled within.

We are embarrassed to think that. Someone loves us so unreservedly without our doing something to deserve it; without us working for it, earning it.

We want to express how we feel but it dribbles off our chin; we're embarrassed to speak in such an intimate, passionate way about Him.

Passion is not something we talk about, especially passion towards the One we cannot see and only know by His indwelling.

Enter the men with the white coats, stage left.

Even among ourselves we temper how we speak of Him.

It's true, isn't it?

We don't want others to think we have gone overboard in this, even our fellow believers.

Odd that.

Weird even.

Because He's not embarrassed to say that we are His passion.

He's not shy about telling us one glance of our eyes has ravished His heart. (Song of Songs 4:9 ASV)

Ravished.

What a word.

What if He were saying over you -

*"I don't see anything wrong with you.*

*All I see is beauty.*

*You are so beautiful.*

*Undefiled.*

*You are a new creation; all the old has passed away.*

*Everything has been new for a long time, you are so **new**; revel in your newness; revel in your cleanness; revel in your purity. I'll help you with all the stuff.*

*I have given you a safe place in My heart.*

*You can adore me because I adore you first.*

*Are you not My beloved?*

*You're Mine, you are Mine. You're My woman. You're My woman. You're clean, pure, and you are beautiful.*

*Permission has been granted for you to live a life overwhelmed."*[1]

Adoration.

Whew!

A famous French woman, Madame Guyon, was reported to have said on one occasion that sometimes her intimacy with the All Mighty was as delicious as a moment of ecstasy with her husband; the statement sent her to the infamous Bastille prison.

Though she used words that sounded as though they were physical, of course she was referring to the spiritual union with her Bridegroom.

Spiritual passion.

His of you; yours of Him.

How's your embarrassment level?

[1] "Soaking in the Beloved", Graham Cooke CD 2009

# 20

# Passion

I left you yesterday asking how your embarrassment level was, sensing that some of you could be feeling a little 'hot under the collar'.

So now we're really getting into it.

Adoration, passion - words we don't usually associate with our relationship with Jesus.

What mind-set change would have to take place in you for these to become the norm?

For you to see whether you are a man or a woman, you are His Bride?

He speaks to you, woos you, with words of love.

Pillow talk…

Words of intimate union.

Not just love, but passion and adoration.

Strong one that, adoration.

Raw, exposed, intimate, passion.

And He isn't apologising.

He speaks in the language of one who is absolutely consumed with the object of His love.

Love, which seeks the best for the object that is loved.

The one whose heart He died to gain.

The one He longs to be with and plans to marry.

His Bride.

Marriage.

Not a concept some in this 21st century embrace.

We have a Kleenex mentality when it comes to the commitment that is required; the covenant that we need to make; to make earthly marriages work through good and bad times.

So we say *"let's have a trial run and see how it works out".*

Trouble is, a few trials, and often several children later, we still haven't found Mr or Mrs Right.

No condemnation, it's just that it isn't like *that* with Him.

He found exactly what He searched for.

He found everything His heart desires, in you.

He's set His love on you.

Not because you are perfect, far from it, but because He loves with Agape, the love of choice; not changing feelings.

**Deuteronomy 10:15.**

Covenant love.

A blood covenant.

No wonder He says, *"Love Me with the love I have given you and that will be enough."* (1 John 4:19 NASB paraphrase)

Got to quote Martin Luther again -

*"Now is this not a happy business? Christ, the rich, noble, and holy bridegroom, takes in marriage this poor, contemptible and sinful little prostitute, takes away all of her evil, and bestows all His goodness upon her! It is no longer possible for sin to overwhelm her, for she is now found in Christ and is swallowed up by Him so that she possesses a rich righteousness in her bridegroom."*

Perhaps we just need to learn to receive the 'much more' of God?

# 21

# Receiving

Receiving, some of us have a great deal of difficulty doing just that.

For some reason when I was thinking and praying about this message, I remembered something about when a child is brought up with criticism.

I wonder if this is the reason so many of us find receiving the unconditional love of God so difficult?

Here it is -

*Dorothy Law Nolte*

*"If a child lives with criticism, he learns to condemn.*

*If a child lives with hostility, he learns to fight.*

*If a child lives with fear, he learns to be apprehensive.*

*If a child lives with pity, he learns to feel sorry for himself.*

*If a child lives with ridicule, he learns to be shy.*

*If a child lives with jealousy, he learns what envy is.*

*If a child lives with shame, he learns to feel guilty.*

*If a child lives with encouragement, he learns to be confident.*

*If a child lives with tolerance, he learns to be patient.*

*If a child lives with praise, he learns to be appreciative.*

*If a child lives with acceptance, he learns to love.*

*If a child lives with approval, he learns to like himself.*

*If a child lives with recognition, he learns that it is good to have a goal.*

*If a child lives with sharing, he learns about generosity.*

*If a child lives with honesty and fairness, he learns what truth and justice are.*

*If a child lives with security, he learns to have faith in himself and in those about him.*

*If a child lives with friendliness, he learns that the world is a nice place in which to live.*

*If you live with serenity, your child will live with peace of mind. With what is your child living?"* [1]

We won't identify with all of these, but I'm sure some of us were brought up with criticism and disapproval, rejection, and exclusion.

This is a legacy from the Fall and is in no way a condemnation of our parents; they did the best they could fallen as they and we, are.

But sometimes we are marked for life by what happened to us as children and when God comes along with His unconditional love it is painful for us to receive; we need reprogramming first.

Jesus promises, if we will let Him, to wash all the damaging effects of the past away for us in order that we can receive His love and affection.

Our problem is that sometimes we just won't *let* Him in.

And we remain almost in an unformed state spiritually.

This is why more of this word could be useful at this point -

*"I'll help you with all the stuff. I have given you a safe place in My heart. You can adore me because I adore you first. Are you not My beloved? You're Mine, you're Mine. You're My woman. You're My woman. You're clean, pure, and you are beautiful."*

*'I'll help you with all the stuff.'* [2]

Won't you let Him do just that?

Help you, with all the stuff?

[1]https://www.bpsd.org/Downloads/Children%20Learn%20What%20They%20Live.pdf

[2] Soaking in the Beloved, CD Graham Cooke

# 22

# Position or performance

And here's another thing; if we are to **abide** in Christ; stay, dwell, and remain, where the Father has placed us; we must be absolutely certain that our behaviour **cannot** disqualify us.

That on a bad day He is not going to say, *"That's it, you've done that once too often, out you go!"*

The reason I say this is that many lovely born-again believers mistake **position** for **performance**.

Saved by grace, they then believe they must now **do** certain things to remain saved, or risk losing their salvation – in other words they must perform, work, for approval.

I have heard it taught many times by many well-known and respected teachers and it is a source of great grief to my heart because it breeds fear in the hearers and a *performance* driven lifestyle rather than a relational lifestyle in Christ.

What they are saying is *"you are saved by grace and then you work to keep it"* or there is a threat of losing your salvation by persistent and wilful wrong behaviour.

They trip up on scriptures such as -

*"The acts of the flesh are obvious: sexual immorality, impurity and debauchery; idolatry and witchcraft; hatred, discord, jealousy, fits of rage, selfish ambition, dissensions, factions and envy; drunkenness, orgies, and the like. I warn you, as I did*

*before, that those who live like this will not inherit the kingdom of God."* (Galatians 5:19-21 NIV)

Here, they confuse salvation with inheritance and the flesh with the Spirit.

They have failed to see that Paul is not talking about salvation, but something very different - inheritance.

He isn't talking about performance, but **position**.

You will see that he interchanges statements such as *"in Christ"* (e.g. Romans 8:1 NIV) and *"in the Lord"* (e.g. Ephesians 6:1 NIV) as you read through the epistles.

When he uses the latter, he is talking about **behavioural** issues.

When he uses the former, he is talking about that which no-man can take from you, the **position** the Father placed you in the moment you believed on His Son.

Salvation is about believing, not performing.

It's about faith, not works.

It's about relationship not religion.

It's about

## GRACE.

Beloved, the way you came in is the way you continue; you are saved by grace and continue to be saved by grace, robed in **His** righteousness alone, you cannot add one act of righteousness, it's all His and it is His delight to give it to you.

Having given it to you, it's called imputed righteousness; He then proceeds to work it in, and this is where inheritance comes in.

You may or may not be willing to let go of the lifestyle you lived before you were saved; you may continue in a wrong sexual relationship, but it isn't going to affect your *position* in Christ; it will affect your inheritance though.

Inheritance is about the amount of Him you can contain - 30, 60, 100%.

As two things cannot occupy the same space, if you persist, for instance, in an adulterous relationship, that part of you isn't under His Lordship. That affects your inheritance - how much of Him you can contain because it is no longer two lives to be lived, but one, and you get to choose how much of Him you want.

You aren't wholehearted in your love and service to Jesus, when something else has a place in your heart and that keeps you in the flesh, which Paul is speaking about here.

So, choices again.

It's entirely up to you, He really will not love you any the less if you persist in doing things contrary to His revealed will; you are the one who will suffer in the end, you won't inherit the Kingdom in this life - love, joy, peace, patience, goodness, self-control and all those good things, and your behaviour means you will forfeit the reward you would otherwise have had when you get to the eternal Kingdom.

If you get nothing else out of this, get this: your salvation is dependent on your **placement** in Christ and that is God's part; your inheritance is dependent on your behavioural choices, and that beloved of God, is your part.

Go in peace whatever you choose.

God *will* bless you; you belong to Him and He can't help Himself!

# 23

# Love relationship

So, once you are in the Kingdom and learning to abide in Christ, it is all about developing that love relationship with Jesus.

The Holy Spirit, who is within you, causes you to lose your taste for the things that are distasteful to Him.

For me an immoral relationship, alcohol dependency and smoking all went within a few weeks of meeting Jesus, almost without my being aware of it.

He didn't threaten or bully me; I just found I had lost my *taste* for those things.

I just didn't *need* them anymore.

The need for alcohol went without any awareness on my part at all...with cigarettes He told me what to do every time I wanted to take one and I haven't smoked from that day to this.

He is so kind.

What am I saying?

Everything and anything He asks you to do, He will **give** you the means to perform. He *never* asks you to do something without showing you how to do it and enabling you to do it.

It all happens out of the depth of His love for you and your reciprocation of that love because, *"we love because He first loved us".* (1 John 4:19 NIV).

When you love someone, you don't want to harm the relationship.

If staying in an adulterous or immoral relationship for instance, would harm my relationship with Jesus, I am going to put a stop to it because He means more to me that that source of satisfaction.

Nobody forces me.

I willingly and unreservedly get rid of that which is in the way because I want nothing to hinder my progress into His great heart.

That is how the love relationship with Him works.

Receiving His love comes first, we talked about that a couple of days ago.

Then the things that consume our thinking and lifestyle will begin to dissolve in the power of His love for us and ours for Him.

He won't *extract* obedience from you.

But He can ask from you, in a time of war, what you gave Him in a time of peace, and usually does.

He will ask for it and then leave you to weigh the consequences of refusal.

He never comes back and says *"I told you so"* when you insist on having your own way and it all goes pear-shaped; instead, He lovingly and patiently lifts you and restores you - just like He did with Peter.

Poor old Peter, so painfully aware of what he had done by denying Jesus three times. Feeling he could never be reinstated his crime was so great, you find the story in **John 21:15** and following - the bible is full of the stories of ordinary people like us, who encountered an extraordinary God who lifted and restored them.

Some unbelievers hold the view that Christians have invented God.

Beloved, no one could dream up Someone as wonderful as He is!

He is beyond our understanding in gentleness, goodness, kindness, faithfulness, and love.

He tenderly cherishes us, encourages us to grow; He never forces or coerces us, but gently leads us as a Shepherd with His lambs.

He is altogether lovely, and certainly not a product of human imagination.

So, how's that love relationship working out for you?

# 24

# That inner compass

This message could be called an object lesson in obedience.

It is so easy to get diverted when writing material like this, or anything else for that matter. The danger is of getting so engrossed in the production I forget **Who** it's all about.

His Majesty.

Jesus.

The greatest threat to your intimacy with God is your work for Him.

Anyone in Christian ministry will know that is the case.

By His grace, I know what it means to leave my first love - the warning He gave to the church at Ephesus. She was commended for her hard work and patience but corrected, because she left her first love and she was called to repent, change her mind. (Revelation 2:4 NIV)

For me it happened like this:

Some months after Oasis had acquired a residential facility for renewal and healing, I had dived deep into the ministry.

It was not unusual for me to start at 10 am and still be going 12 hours later.

I would probably still be there had not the Lord called a *very* sudden and abrupt halt to proceedings.

When something like that happens, we really need to know and understand His ways; anything, I mean anything - particularly 'good' things that take our attention and focus away from Him - He will remove from our lives.

He is life's summum bonum, not what we do.

And He has ways of teaching us and keeping us focussed.

In my particular instance I was in the healing ministry; I had a diary of appointments three months ahead when He told me one morning to stop immediately; cancel everything and take 21 days out.

Very clear instruction.

It was not popular with those who had appointments, but then I wasn't called to win a popularity contest, but to follow Him.

In obedience I took myself off to the home of a friend in Devon.

On the first day of the retreat, for that was what I subsequently discovered it was, I was browsing idly in a charity shop, asking in my heart why I was there, when I pulled out a sweatshirt - emblazoned across the front were the words

### *'First Love'*

Immediately I knew why I had had to cancel everything. I had got my eyes off Him, and on to the needs of the people; the work He had called me to do.

The ministry had become more of a priority to me than my relationship with Him.

The greatest threat to my intimacy *with* God was my work *for* Him.

Needs, for those of you in ministry, never go away, they will always be with you, like the poor.

The good is the enemy of the best.

The best was my pursuit of *Him*.

What I discovered from this sharp lesson was that it is from that place of intimacy with Him, that work and ministry flows.

When I put Him first, everything else trots along behind like the tail of a dog.

I have never forgotten He requires my unshared love and attention *before* anything and everything else as a result I ensure that my inner compass is always set on true North.

He is my lodestar.

I put Him first before any needs that arise, and following the Master, I only do what I see the Father doing and only say what He is saying.

It's called radical obedience, and total dependency.

Radical obedience + total dependency = a place of abiding.

When we follow the Maker's instructions, loving Him first with all our heart, soul, mind, and strength, recognising that the Kingdom the power and the glory are His alone and we simply love Him as we are commanded to do, we find we are about ready to love our neighbour.

But not before.

It has to be the right way up.

Love the Lord; then your neighbour; then everything else falls into place.

You know what's coming - how's it working out for you?

# 25

# When I do not love God

I can almost hear the wail from some of you, *"But I don't love God, I don't know how to"*.

Number one on this is that He **never** asks you to do anything that doesn't originate with Him.

I'll say that again differently - He always gives you first what He asks for.

So, we love, because He first loved us. (1 John 4:19 NIV).

First love.

He did it.

We simply reciprocate with what we have already been given.

For those of you struggling with the first commandment, there's your answer in a nutshell.

You can't love Him until you have **received** His agape love for you.

When you have, you find loving Him isn't difficult, and loving your neighbour comes naturally.

Well, supernaturally naturally really.

Because agape love, the love of choice, that He sets upon you and you return to Him, is not natural love.

It is the love of choice that bypasses whether the object of that love *deserves* it or not.

One of our main problems as human beings is that we operate on the unwritten rule that people *deserve* what they get.

'Fess up now.

Examine your heart.

*"You deserved that."*

*"You don't deserve that, but I'm giving it to you anyway".*

Anyone who has had a child will know those phrases well.

There is a way in which they must earn it, whatever 'it' is, be it a reward for good behaviour or your love and acceptance.

It's called **conditional** love and approval.

I will love you and approve of you on these conditions - tick the boxes or not as appropriate; if you do not meet my expectations, forget it.

Living under conditional love can mar us for life.

I did and it affected me all my life until He taught me what love was.

This is why He gave us a new heart; and a new DNA, a new start, so we could learn what love is *really* all about.

God's love is so superabundantly higher than ours, that when we begin to receive it we can't believe it, it is too good to be true; but once we receive it we can't help passing it on to the good, the bad and the ugly around us, no one is safe from a blessing.

They don't have to do anything to deserve it; we just want to love and bless them; it just happens.

That's how the Kingdom works.

And this is how you can know if you are living the love of God and giving it away. You cease judging and weighing; comparing and criticising; and you just unconditionally love everyone, in the same way you are loved.

You understand suddenly, what it is like to be in their shoes.

You identify with them.

Now Someone else did that…identified.

[1] *'Christ has regarded my helpless estate and has shed His own blood for my soul.'*

You become like Jesus.

The more room you allow Him, the more of Himself He will pour into you.

That is what the Kingdom of God is.

His nature in exchange for yours.

His reign and rule in your life and emotions, instead of yours.

Could be good.

Why not give it a try?

Just tell Him you've had enough of doing it your way and want to do it His way.

It's called *"Thy Kingdom come, Thy will be done"*. (Matthew 6:10 KJV).

Simple as falling off a log…

---

[1] *'When peace like a river'* Songwriters: Philip Paul Bliss / Christopher C. C. Stafford 'It Is Well with My Soul' lyrics © Warner/Chappell Music, Inc, Universal Music Publishing Group

26

# Keeping the main thing
# the main thing

So what's the main thing?

Keeping a right view of His Majesty, and His ownership of us.

Not allowing the pursuit of getting our needs met, our prayers answered, or our ministry, to overshadow His glory.

Because Who **He** is must be the main thing.

He is GOOD.

It always comes back to the first commandment; love Him first with the love He gives you. So, we cannot avoid intimacy - because love is about relationship.

We can run but we cannot hide.

He will track us down and like Elijah He will ask *'What are you doing here?'* (1 Kings 19:9 NIV)

All Elijah's physical needs were met; he was fed and watered; he went to sleep and was rested; Jesus knows how to look after His sheep.

He makes the sun shine on the righteous and the unrighteous alike.

He provides for all.

He prepared the garden *before* He created man and put him in it.

Everything man would need was there.

Nothing lacking.

He can be trusted.

Therein lies profound truth - He can be trusted.

He is the Creator we, are the created.

But for many of us the instinct to preserve ourselves; protect ourselves; nurture ourselves; provide for ourselves; in other words, our desire for *self*-rule and preservation, is so strong and deeply rooted that when He comes and says, *"move over darling"*, we are surprised at what He reveals to us of the ways in which we have bastioned ourselves against His advances.

We are like a fortified city.

High walls.

Drawbridge.

Portcullis.

Or a Martello tower, which is a defensive fort; out of which we look with suspicion upon anyone who seeks to enter. Our greatest foe, you will have realised by now, is not Satan, but the person who looks back at you from the mirror. *"We have seen the enemy and he is us"*, someone so rightly said.

*"Self is the only prison that can bind the soul."* (Attributed to Henry Van Dyke.)

We are our own worst enemy. Like our Federal head, Adam, we are suspicious of God's motives towards us. And maybe our first step towards the restoration of wholeness starts when we admit this to ourselves and then to Him and begin the long journey back by allowing Him to know what is best for us.

The journey of a thousand miles starts with the first step.

# 27

# Prodigal God

We commenced this section talking about the Holy Spirit's role, which is primarily to glorify Jesus.

*"When He comes",* Jesus said, *"He will tell you about the things of Me and glorify Me."* (John 16:13,14 NIV paraphrase)

This is what is meant by keeping the main thing the main thing.

We must never forget that we are on our way somewhere…and Jesus is our Way, our map.

Of necessity we must stay close to Him, or we will lose our way.

If we stray away from Jesus as our 'main thing', we find ourselves in all sorts of difficulties.

He alone is our true magnetic North.

The Father has placed us in heavenly places *in Him*.

He has assigned us a place specific to each of us in His Son; and it is from **there** that we are meant to grow spiritually and affect the things on the earth - for good.

We are citizens of another kingdom; this world is not our home.

We are in the short-stay car park here.

We need reminding, don't we?

If we are not vigilant, the joy and liberation we felt when we were first saved dissipates and dissolves into routine married life, and just like the church at Ephesus, we find it easy to wander away from our first love. (Revelation 2:4 NKJV)

Many of us I suspect *'made a commitment'*, *'became a Christian'* or even *'accepted Christ'* years ago but the reality was that you did none of those things. What happened was God sovereignly drew you; revealed your need of a Saviour to you and you responded, as you saw your true situation; without Jesus you were eternally damned.

Beloved you were 'saved'.

You were saved *from* something *to* something.

You were saved from the wrath to come and from yourself.

The wrath to come - that's something we don't like to think about, particularly if we hold the view that everyone will 'be all right in the end'.

Plain fact is, they won't be.

The day of reckoning will come.

The day when every unbeliever will stand before the Great White Throne and give an account for him or herself of how they have lived their lives. They will have to do that because they never received God's free gift of salvation, so the penalty for their sin remains unpaid.

It's a bit like a parking fine; you will have to pay it sooner or later, unless of course, someone steps in and pays it for you - that is exactly what Jesus did and we accepted that offer, so we will never stand before the throne of judgement.

He was judged and the was penalty paid by Him and we went off scot-free.

It's easy to forget isn't it:

*"Oh to grace how great a debtor,*

*Daily I'm constrained to be, let that grace Lord like a fetter,*

*Bind my wandering heart to Thee,*

*Prone to wander, Lord I feel it,*

*Prone to leave the God I love, take my heart,*

*O take and seal it, seal from Thy courts above."*[1]

We have short-term memory loss and that is why the Father gave us the precious gift of the Holy Spirit to indwell us to keep us in remembrance of His great grace towards us.

We were also saved from *ourselves* and our old sin nature, as by baptism, we entered resurrection life in Christ.

You did understand that didn't you?

When you went through the waters of immersion you rose in newness of life, the old having been left behind, that is the significance of it. It's not just an opportunity for a tea party; it marks a rite of passage from the old life to the new.

It is interesting that the closer we get to Him the more astonished and amazed we are and the more we marvel.

Maybe that is a yardstick for you this day - if you aren't astonished and amazed any more, it is time to retrace your steps and see where you lost your way.

The Father will be waiting for His prodigal to return, of that you can be absolutely sure.

---

[1] *'Come Thou fount of every blessing'* hymn by Robert Robinson

# 28

# From and to

I said yesterday that we were saved from something to something.

You were saved from the lake of fire, into the eternal kingdom of the Son of God; from the kingdom of darkness, into the Kingdom of Light. And from your self-life into His life.

That is what you are saved from and to.

You aren't saved just to go to heaven, but to live a productive life here whilst on earth, and then to reign and rule with Him for eternity.

You were saved from yourself into resurrection life in Christ.

Because God plans for eternity.

I have said it before; nothing is an afterthought with Him.

He isn't standing up there biting His nails, full of anxiety in case we don't pray correctly for what He wants to do.

He is the Sovereign Ruler of the Universe; the Creator of *all* things, not just some, and He holds all things together by the word of His power -

*"Going through a long line of prophets, God has been addressing our ancestors in different ways for centuries. Recently he spoke to us directly through his Son. By his Son, God created the world in the beginning, and it will all belong to*

*the Son at the end. This Son perfectly mirrors God, and is stamped with God's nature. He holds everything together by what he says—powerful words!"* (Hebrews 1:1-3 The Message)

In Him you live and move and have your being. (Acts 17:28 NKJV),

Hard one I know, but you draw your next breath because His word goes forth and sustains you.

Now that's something to thank Him for right there!

Alignment is something we need to look at from time to time because it is so very easy to get out of alignment, out of focus, and find ourselves losing that eternal perspective.

Let me give you God's upcoming events: the next major date on His calendar is the catching away of His bride, or the Rapture as it is sometimes called.

Sorry if you thought the next event was the Second Coming, it isn't, the next event could be much closer than you think; He could come while you are reading this - now there's a thought.

Have you ever taken time to consider the parable of the wise and the foolish virgins?

The doctrine of imminency, which is what I am talking about, is something we rarely hear about these days; it isn't popular; thinking about our eternal state isn't popular either; locked as we are into the here and now.

There is a Satanic strategy to keep you earth-bound in your thinking beloved, living in the old nature not the new.

God wants you fit and ready for His Son when He comes to collect His bride.

That is what all these messages are about, a thinly disguised attempt to prepare your heart for your Bridegroom and your meeting with Him.

193

Your Father plans for eternity - from the Garden of Eden He has been seeking a bride for His Son, one who will love Him and who will be a fit companion for Him.

Beloved you have an astonishing future ahead of you, of which currently we only have a glimpse.

You have been chosen with all foreknowledge to be presented to Him on that Day as His glorious Bride and co-regent for eternity.

That was *not* Adam's inheritance.

But it is yours.

Makes it worth taking stock of where you are and what your priorities are doesn't it?

When we get an eternal perspective, everything else pales into insignificance as we stand open mouthed in wonder that the Creator of the Universe should set His love upon us in such a way and want us to share everything that He has.

That's what it is.

He wants us to be a part of the Eternal Godhead.

Part of the community of Heaven; that which was always been and will always be; now *that* is some inheritance and surely something to look forward to.

# 29

# Son everything I have is yours

The father in the lovely story of the prodigal son, said this -

*"Son, everything I have is yours"*. (Luke 15:31 NIV)

The significance of this can easily miss us.

What He is saying to us is *"everything is yours in My Son and I have placed you in Him so that you might inherit all things"*.

As a born-again believer, twice-born from earth and from heaven, you are now enclosed and embraced by the Son of God by the Divine fiat of the Father.

He spoke the word and you were placed *in* His Son. (cf Ephesians 2:6 NASB).

That gives you all the rights and privileges that pertain to Jesus; it means Father loves you in exactly same way, as He loves His Son.

New to you?

I'll let that sink in for a moment.

So when in psalm 2:8 He says *"Ask Me and I will give you the nations for an inheritance"*, He is saying the same thing to you.

"Ask Me".

We are given unbelievable access to the Throne-room of God where we can petition according to His will. Like Jesus we can come to the place where we only do what we see the Father doing and only say what we hear Him saying…

*"In this is love, not that we loved God, but that He loved us and sent His Son to be the propitiation for our sins. Beloved, if God so loved us, we also ought to love one another. No one has seen God at any time; if we love one another, God abides in us, and His love is perfected in us. By this we know that we abide in Him and He in us, because He has given us of His Spirit. We have seen and testify that the Father has sent the Son to be the Saviour of the world. Whoever confesses that Jesus is the Son of God, God abides in him, and he in God. We have come to know and have believed the love which God has for us. God is love, and the one who abides in love abides in God, and God abides in him. By this, love is perfected with us, so that we may have confidence in the day of judgment; because as He is, so also are we in this world."* (1 John 4:17-19 NKJV)

*"As He is, in this world, so are we."*

We are learning to love as Jesus loved - notice that love is the motivator in all of this - and we are learning to be exactly the same as He is, in this present darkness.

But like everything else, it is incremental.

This is why I keep reminding you that you can have as much of Him as you really, really want.

If you desire it, He will give you *all* of Himself.

Which will mean that all of *you* will have to go, because two things cannot occupy the same space.

But you are planning and storing up for eternity; you aren't locked into 70 odd years here and nothing to follow.

You have an *eternal* inheritance, and an *eternal* life to look forward to, so question, in which realm **are** you currently investing?

Here or eternity.

Those two realities again.

Earthly or heavenly.

You get to choose.

He isn't going to love you any the less.

Everything He has is yours.

It is there for the asking, but you need to draw near, ask, receive, and then give away what you get.

What God holds out to us are His exceedingly great and precious promises, but to come into them will require us to develop a heart and mind-set that reveres, honours, and respects Him for Who He is, as well as a heart that is fully engaged in an intimate relationship with Him.

His Majesty.

Just imagine what emotions you might feel if Charles III, the King of England called you and invited you have an intimate relationship with him; to be his friend and confidante and more, to reign with him.

If an earthly monarch's invitation would cause your heart to skip a beat, how much more should your heart be amazed and marvel at what the King of kings and Lord of lords holds out to you.

The only proper response is to bow the knee; touch the sceptre; and accept His most gracious of offers.

Doing that, beloved, will take you into the realm of which dreams are made.

# 30

# The Secret Place

We are fast approaching the end of our journey into looking at what living a Kingdom lifestyle looks like.

Our last and maybe most important session is about living in the Secret Place. - psalm 91 refers.

Living from there is the springboard to your identity and your destiny.

It is where you will learn how God sees you and what He plans for you.

What you will need to become to fulfil that plan.

The Secret Place of God's own heart.

Embedded in Psalm 91.

You may want take a look at it right now…

We will see what life looks like when we live our lives *participating* in the Christ, not just *imitating* Him; living from the place Jesus died to give us.

We will see that there is an acceleration possible, should you wish to avail yourself of it.

You will begin to understand the battle we are in and how to remain standing when everything around us is crumbling and falling apart.

How you can make your circumstances subject to you rather than be controlled by them…

Living in the place that Jesus died to give you.

We have come a long way and yet it seems we have hardly travelled at all.

As with everything in the Christian life, God loves to tell us something and then make it real to us as we experience it.

A man with an experience, it has been said, is beyond reason.

No one can reason with us when we have really met with the Lord.

No one can reason with us when we have really decided to follow Jesus.

No one can reason with us when we become disciples.

No one can reason with us when we get a revelation of where we are and who we are in the Christ and where we are going.

We are the ones who will turn the world upside down. (cf Acts 17:6).

So, the conclusion of the matter.

We have decided to follow Jesus now and we know what it means be disciples, not believers or followers, but disciples.

Permanent learners.

Apprenticed to the Master.

Always receiving greater revelation of what a great God we serve.

# Experiencing God

*"Aslan is a lion - the Lion, the great Lion." "Ooh" said Susan. "I'd thought he was a man. Is he - quite safe? I shall feel rather nervous about meeting a lion"..."Safe?" said Mr Beaver ..."Who said anything about safe? 'Course he isn't safe. But he's good. He's the King, I tell you."*

The Lion, the witch and the wardrobe' C S Lewis.

# 1

# Roll over or pushover

This is where our journey into God's great heart really begins and where it starts to get interesting; we are about to move from theory to practice and the pace will slow.

God loves to make what we have learned in the classroom *real* in our experience.

So, we get to experience Him, a practical.

This is where we learn whether we are those who roll over in that we submit happily to God without murmuring or dissenting; or whether, by our choices, or resistance, we have become a pushover for the enemy.

If it is the latter, we are immediately out from the place Father put us in, we are in Satan's territory, and he will make every use of it.

We need first and foremost to become nodding dogs. By that I mean we learn to say 'Yes Lord', even before He asks the question. Incidentally you cannot say 'No' and 'Lord' in the same sentence. If you are refusing Him or stonewalling Him, He isn't Lord.

So, everything we have learned so far is now going to be tested in the school of life.

We are going to find out what it means truly to love one another; the hard way or the easy way, we get to choose; what it means to die to ourselves, ditto; what it means to lay down our lives for others ditto; preferring others and so on.

Life in the Spirit you will recall, is about displacement.

Jesus didn't come to make us healthy, wealthy, and wise no matter what some may tell you.

He modelled something for us; self-giving love; agape, the love of choice.

The Father's intention is to bring many *sons* to glory.

Not many babes in arms.

This is why we need to ask ourselves if we are a believer, a follower, or a disciple.

By now you will know there is a difference.

Believers believe for a time and then fall away; followers usually follow until He or someone else offends them; disciples keep going on and learning. Setting their faces as flint, they do as He says - *'never mind about what anybody else is doing, you follow Me'.* (John 21:22 NKJV)

That said, there might have been a fall-out already.

But if you are up for the climb, I will see you tomorrow.

2

# Lord we have left all

*"When Jesus heard this, He said to him, "One thing you still lack; sell all that you possess and distribute it to the poor, and you shall have treasure in heaven; and come, follow Me." But when he had heard these things, he became very sad, for he was extremely rich. And Jesus looked at him and said, "How hard it is for those who are wealthy to enter the kingdom of God! For it is easier for a camel to go through the eye of a needle than for a rich man to enter the kingdom of God."* (Luke 18:22-25 NASB)

At first glance it may look as though Jesus is against people who are wealthy, but this isn't the case, you only need to look at Abraham, David and Solomon, exceedingly rich people, so He must be getting at something else.

You will know by now that what He is getting at is the heart.

This young man had an idol in his heart, and that was his wealth.

As two things could not possibly occupy the same place, Jesus tells him to sell all he has which elicited the response of sorrow, *'for he was extremely rich'.*

I spoke yesterday about 'dying' to ourselves and mentioned several things such as loving others; dying to ourselves simply means that we are no longer focussed on our own needs but

205

have transferred our concerns to the needs of those around us, placing them first in our priority list, not ourselves.

We are effectively dethroned as Jesus takes the throne of our lives for real and proceeds to show us what we can live without.

There is the wry tale of an old Puritan who watched a neighbour moving in all his goods and was overheard to call out to him - *'friend, when thou hast finished come and see me and I will tell thee how thou canst do without all that stuff...'*

Stuff.

Some spend their lives on the acquisition of it, and should the Lord say *'I want you to get rid of that'* it is as though their very arm had been severed, so attached are they to it.

So we need to look at some kingdom laws to end our time together.

The first of which could be called the law of letting go, of relinquishment, so we relate differently to people and things close to us. To understand this concept, we need to grasp the fact that we steward everything in this life and own nothing. Not our house, our wives or husbands, our children, our money, our gifts; everything has been given to us by God, who owns all things.

We simply *steward* everything.

And a steward takes care of something until the owner shows up, and when he does, the steward shows how he has taken care of that which was entrusted to him; whatever it is, it never belonged to him, ever.

It was on loan to him.

So we have to learn to relate differently to everything and everyone around us and in so doing, we experience God as He really, really is, not the God of our self-indulgent imagination.

No longer holding on tight to money, job, car, house, spouse, children, or stuff, we release it all into the hand of Him who gave it and begin our journey of transformation; renewal of our minds; in the way we perceive and think about our possessions and everything else besides.

It is the way to freedom.

That is what Romans 12:1-2 is talking about.

I'll leave you to look that one up and think about and we'll continue tomorrow.

# 3

# I am a jealous God

The 'I Am' is a jealous God. (Exodus 20:5 NIV).

He is jealous for our unshared love and affection because unless our love is changed and transformed, it is human love, human kindness, human generosity and all our good deeds are not good at all because they do not stem from the only One who is Good, God Himself, they come from our lower, fallen nature.

Ouch.

Hear His opinion of our 'good' deeds:

*'But we are all like an unclean thing,*
*And all our righteousnesses are like filthy rags;'* (Isaiah 64:6 NKJV)

If you would like to know what filthy rags are, they are, literally, menstrual cloths; doesn't get much more graphic than that beloved; that's how He sees anything that is tainted with the natural man, the flesh, the lower nature.

It stinks.

Remember Cain?

He brought the work of his hands.

Sweaty effort.

Abel gave God what He asked for - blood - in the form of a lamb from the flock.

A type and shadow of the Lamb of God who would be given to restore and reconcile all men to God, should they choose to accept it.

So, back to the script - jealousy.

Even our goodness and kindness, has to die so that His Majestic love can take its place.

It all has to go *because* He has won a new start and a completely new beginning for us on the Cross.

We are **new creations**, in the Christ.

If we don't come into that we nullify His finished work.

So, what we are talking about here, among other things, is ownership; specifically His jealous right to what He owns.

Us.

Blood bought believers.

Bought from the slave-market of sin and transferred into the Kingdom of light.

Ownership has changed.

Ownership changed the moment you believed on the Son of God's perfect sacrifice on your behalf.

No longer two lives now, but one.

His.

In you, and then through you.

Basic theology.

He is God.

You are not.

He is on the throne of your life.

You are not.

Be gone self-rule, independence; out black spot!

Talking about sin - which is what self-rule is - and how it permeates our whole being to the point where we are totally unaware of It A W Tozor puts it like this:

*"A moral being, created to worship before the Throne of God, sits on the throne of his own selfhood and from that elevated position declares 'I AM'."* [1]

Furthermore, he goes on to say, *"That is sin in its concentrated essence, yet because it is natural, it appears good"*; it is the ultimate rebellion of which we are largely unaware, even though we may have been Christians for many years, the desire for self-rule.

Our desire to keep self-rule; independence; and self-government.

When God comes to change all that - it will hit you, my beloved, right where you live.

But it is done because He loves you with a passion.

Jealously.

And He wants the very **best** for the object of His love.

Which is of course, Himself.

Nothing more, nothing less.

[1] 'The Knowledge of the Holy', A W Tozer, Harper Collins, 1961 pp29,30

# 4

# The fish tank

You remember of course, the man with the fish tank, how could you ever forget such a graphic example of God asking for something that was dear to the heart.

In case you have only just joined us, the man loved his fish tank.

Tropical fish they were, beautiful.

In a large, expensive, and very well-equipped tank.

Every night after work he would sit back and relax, gazing lovingly at his fish; the day came when God said, *'I'll have that'* - please keep in mind we give Him in a time of peace what He extracts in a time of war - and the poor man was decimated as Father said *'Down the toilet with the fish, and get rid of the tank too'.*

The moral of the tale of course is that these fish had a place in the man's heart that God Himself was jealous to occupy. (see James 4:5)

He is a God who is jealous over you - did you realise that?

If you did, did you realise He really, really means it?

He never speaks idle words.

He is *so* intentional towards us.

In fact, when His intentionality catches up with us, it clean takes our breath away.

Because then we really begin to see Him as He is; and understand who and Whose we are.

Brilliant.

But change is here to stay.

Everything is now under His microscope.

No stone will remain unturned.

Everything is up for grabs.

Fine if you are someone who rolls over with your paws in the air and submits to His Lordship - all good; not so good if you are a resister, or worse.

But you get to choose, so that's all right.

It's never too late to turn.

Never too late to learn.

Never too late to let go.

Never too late to lay down your arms and surrender to His.

# 5

# His ways

Isaiah says that the ways of God are not our ways, and he says it like this - God speaking through the mouth of the prophet -

*"For My thoughts are not your thoughts,*
*Nor are your ways My ways," says the Lord.*
*"For as the heavens are higher than the earth,*
*So are My ways higher than your ways,*
*And My thoughts than your thoughts.*
*"For as the rain comes down, and the snow from heaven,*
*And do not return there,*
*But water the earth,*
*And make it bring forth and bud,*
*That it may give seed to the sower*
*And bread to the eater,*
*So shall My word be that goes forth from My mouth;*
*It shall not return to Me void,*
*But it shall accomplish what I please,*
*And it shall prosper in the thing for which I sent it."* (Isaiah 55:8-11 NKJV)

That, in essence, explains it.

Everything comes from Him and goes back to Him.

We think that He thinks the same way as we do and we are terribly wrong, take a look at Psalm 50:21 sometime - *'You thought I was altogether like you...'* you thought wrong! (My version.)

This causes everything from our being offended by what He says; to us walking away altogether; we simply do not understand His ways.

But if we would take just a little time studying how He has related to His people from Genesis to Revelation, we would see the High and Holy One as He really, really is, and be amazed, astonished, and marvel.

We might even develop something that is sadly lacking in this 21st century, fear of the Lord, which is the beginning of wisdom. (Proverbs 9:10 NIV). He is good and He is altogether lovely, and His ways are past finding out; He is to be revered, honoured, feared, loved, awed and admired, by those He calls His children.

One thing of which we can be sure, He is always just when He speaks and blameless when He judges - king David found this out when he sinned with Bathsheba and had her husband murdered.

Hear what he was moved to say when God sent another prophet, Nathan, to him to bring him to repentance -

*"Have mercy upon me, O God,*
*According to Your lovingkindness;*
*According to the multitude of Your tender mercies,*
*Blot out my transgressions.*
*Wash me thoroughly from my iniquity,*
*And cleanse me from my sin.*

*For I acknowledge my transgressions,*
*And my sin is always before me.*
*Against You, You only, have I sinned,*
*And done this evil in Your sight—*
*That You may be found just when You speak,*
*And blameless when You judge."* (Psalm 51:1-4 NKJV)

It is the **goodness** of God that leads us to repent; change our minds; hearts and behaviour in that order -

*"Do the riches of his extraordinary kindness make you take him for granted and despise him? Haven't you experienced how kind and understanding he has been to you? Don't mistake his tolerance for acceptance. Do you realise that all the wealth of his extravagant kindness is meant to melt your heart and lead you into repentance?"* (Romans 2:4)

Beloved, we must know and experience Him as He is, the Holy One of Israel; high and lifted up and His train fills the Temple; Isaiah again. (see Isaiah 6:1)

When we see Him, we cannot but be like Job, repent in dust and ashes. (Job 42:6 NIV)

If we haven't repented and kept on repenting every day of our lives - by this I mean changing our view and understanding of Him - I question whether we are making any spiritual growth at all.

We are meant to live in continuous repentance, changing of our minds, as we acknowledge that we aren't as clever as we thought we were and that He is the all knowing, all seeing and all sustaining One, who is altogether lovely.

And we magnify Him and love His ways with us.

# 6

# Thinking differently

Bob Mumford has written a lovely book, which I highly recommend; the title is *'The King and You'*. In it he talks about the Kingdom, what it is and what it isn't, and how God has to change the way we think and look at things. He calls it re-relating, as he too, travels through the Sermon on the Mount.

The point he makes is, as I have already said; we need to learn to relate differently to everything once we become a Christian.

We need to be de-centred.

By that I mean, removed from sitting on the throne of our lives, to the place where we allow Him to reign.

The reason being we are all **self**-centred.

We are constantly focussed on how everything affects us.

Like a baby, everything revolves around getting **our** needs met; how things makes us feel or how they affects our lives.

When the Holy Spirit comes to take up residence, He begins the long haul to bring us into alignment with the Father.

The way He thinks, feels, and sees things.

It is a huge *perspective* change.
It means a radical adjustment on our part.

A definite move of the feet, or He will tread right on our toes.

He is gentle, but He won't let up.

His government has invaded our lives and we are no longer reigning.

Sorry about that.

There is another King.

His purpose is to conform *you* to the image of Jesus.

This is the Father's goal and stated intent for your life, that you might become like His Son; from the inside out.

He doesn't go in for a paint and wallpaper makeover, but attacks the very foundations.

The reason is twofold: 1) we are called to be His ambassadors and an ambassador reflects and represents the country from which he was sent; and 2) we are training for reigning.

We no longer belong to this world, but we are citizens of a heavenly kingdom and unless this becomes a reality, we will find ourselves at odds with the Holy Spirit all the time and inner conflict will be the norm.

What is hitting is the reality of the heavenly rebirth.

It isn't just so you can say you will go to heaven when you die; you are now in boot camp, training for reigning in a Kingdom that will never end.

Jesus is the embodiment of the Kingdom; He is our pattern and to enable us to rise to where He sits, we have the indwelling Holy Spirit to teach us.

Time to enjoy this journey of development and change, and remember, pain *is* sometimes part of the transformation – how much depends on your level of resistance.

It's entirely up to you.

This thing can be relatively painless, should you choose, by embracing the change, not resisting it.

Entirely up to you.

# 7

# He is circular

God is circular.

By that I mean everything begins with Him and ends with Him and we are somewhere in the middle -

*"Oh, the depth of the riches both of the wisdom and knowledge of God! How unsearchable are His judgments and His ways past finding out!*

*"For who has known the mind of the Lord?*
*Or who has become His counsellor?"*
*"Or who has first given to Him*
*And it shall be repaid to him?"*

*For of Him and through Him and to Him are all things, to whom be glory forever. Amen."* (Romans 11:33-36 NKJV)

That is commonly known as the doxology - or 'glory' word.

*"Of Him and through Him and to Him - all things…"*

Not some things.

***All*** *things.*

We do well to remember this.

Nothing comes to us except He allows it because it must pass through Him.

All the plans of the enemy are wrapped up in the hand of our Friend.

Bonus.

If He allows a situation, it will be for our profit, upgrade, increase, training or equipping - and will turn to profit for us provided we approach it properly.

Yahoo!

So, we can give thanks in all circumstances, (1 Thessalonians 5:18 NIV), the good, the bad and the ugly, because God has a purpose in allowing them.

That is when we experience Him - for real.

When we can say *'All this is true, yet I worship You'*; we're in lamentation – everything's falling apart, but I acknowledge Who You are in it all; His Majesty, full of grace and truth.

We see there is a 'though' and a 'yet'. (Habakkuk 3:17–19)

This is probably our hardest lesson of all in relinquishment.

Everything has gone pear shaped; we are flat on the floor, hopeless and helpless; He alone is our help.

And that is when we find this out.

When He is all you have, you discover He is all you need.

Not a word for the fainthearted.

But it will transform a wimp into a warrior if it is taken to heart.

# 8

# You are all I need

We were talking yesterday about knowing that God was all we needed, and we only find this out when He is all we have.

Sometimes He must allow circumstances to bring us to the end of ourselves before we will willingly relinquish our demands for Him to do things the way we want them done. I'm sure you have experienced that in some measure in your own life.

We cry out for Him to answer prayer in a particular way and the heavens are brass.

We think He doesn't hear or is unwilling to help.

We rail, we plead, we bargain, and finally we accede.

*'You win.'*

In His kindness, He leaves us alone in order that we discover that He *does* know best, and what we were pleading for so importunately wasn't His best.

What we were clamouring for wasn't what He wanted us to have.

We were missing Him.

It is at that point we begin to **experience** Him.

And for some it is extremely inconvenient, not to say, painful.

Many people confuse experiencing God with a warm feeling of being loved and enwrapped, that's right and lovely; you always wrap a babe in something warm and soft. However, as the infant grows, you begin to train it. It is at this point, if we are locked into the 'warm fuzzy', we experience something akin to a cold shower as He begins to conform us to the image of His Son and life becomes distinctly uncomfortable.

We discover that we could get away with putting our breakfast bowl on our heads when we were nine months old, but now we are ten, it won't be tolerated.

Just good, normal, healthy, child training.

It may come as somewhat of a shock, to be told that all the circumstances around your life right now are compatible with His will, because everything can be used for profit.

There are no 'loss' accounts in heaven. Only profit.

So, it behoves us to find out what He is endeavouring to teach us in our current circumstances, in order that we may grow thereby -

*Suffering and Glory*

*"Beloved friends, if life gets extremely difficult, with many tests, don't be bewildered as though something strange were overwhelming you. Instead, continue to rejoice, for you, in a measure, have shared in the sufferings of the Anointed One so that you can share in the revelation of his glory and celebrate with even greater gladness! If you are insulted because of the name of Christ, you are greatly blessed, because the Spirit of glory and power, who is the Spirit of God, rests upon you.*

*Let none of you merit suffering as a murderer, or thief, or criminal, or as one who meddles in the affairs of others. If you suffer for being a Christian, don't consider it a disgrace but a privilege. Glorify God because you carry the Anointed One's name. For the time is ripe for judgment to begin in God's own household. And if it starts with us, what will be the fate of those who refuse to obey the gospel of God?"* (1 Peter 4:12-17)

It is interesting how Peter differentiates suffering - don't suffer as a murderer, a thief or a criminal, and links it with meddling in the affairs of others; that is something most of us do understand. We meddle, or we try to.

'Fess up you wives.

You meddle in your husband's life (or lack of it) with the Lord.

And you suffer for it don't you?

Why not take Pete's advice and stop it?

Cut both of you some slack.

Two-word counsel - stop it!

And learn the lesson Father is trying to teach you.

Love him where he is.

# 9

# By experience

In Pentecostal and Charismatic circles, we hear much about *'the anointing'*. It is something to be experienced, sought after and revered.

We don't go very far into John's gospel before we see what it is.

*'The Son can do nothing of Himself'*. (John 5:17-30 NKJV)

*'The works I do are not mine'*.

As we **experience** God, it will happen just as Jesus describes.

*'All of You and none of me.'*

*'The Son can do nothing of Himself'.*

Jesus, completely and utterly yielded to the Father's will in everything, admits that in His humanity, He can do nothing of Himself.

It isn't any different for us.

There is no fame, glory, no reputation for us - **all** the glory is His.

The anointing is the indwelling Presence.

And He cannot do *through* you what He hasn't been able to do *in* you.

It's a principle.

We can do nothing unless He himself does it **through** us, as vessels completely yielded to Him allowing His life to flow through us without let or hindrance.

Doesn't compute to the natural mind.

Helpless.

Useless.

Yielded.

We wait.

If He doesn't come and do it, it won't get done.

It's not a pleasant experience.

People are looking at you and to you.

And nothing happens.

Zilch.

Nada.

Nothing.

*"Now would be a good time Lord..."* dribbles off the end of our chin.

The loss of our natural strength, the self-life is a necessity because the anointing carries with it the absolute Lordship of Jesus Christ.

In the words of John the Baptist, *'It is necessary for him to increase, and for me to decrease'*. (John 3:30).

Not just words beloved if you seek to experience God as He really, really is.

It will be **all** Him.

[1] *"Day by day His tender mercy,*
*Healing, helping, full and free,*
*Sweet and strong and ah, so patient,*
*Brought me lower while I whispered,*
*"Less of self and more of Thee."*

The way up is down.

He has this series of elegant tests that take us lower each time.

He must increase.

Self-serving must go; you are coming to the place where you fear elevation because you know what is inside you; and the predisposition to take the praise to yourself evaporates.

*'For I know that in me dwells no good thing...'* (Romans 7:18 paraphrase)

We say we love Him, but we like to have *some* recognition; *some* of our own way as well; a little credit...?

No condemnation.

Reality.

*'I delight to do Your will O my God'.* (Psalm 40:8 TPT)

Little way to go yet then.

He's finding us out.

But He knew already; it was we who didn't know ourselves.

He brings us into loving subjection to Himself.

This isn't about you being squashed but about Him being pre-eminent.

We take our worth from Him.

We come into everything He won on the cross by submission to the Divine will.

His Lordship over us, letting Him have the pre-eminence.

The Lordship of Jesus is not something that strips us, takes everything from us or keeps us down so we dare not move. On the contrary, it frees us from the tyranny of the self-life.

The Lordship of the Spirit brings us into fullness of His headship...*'of His fullness we have all received'.* (John 1:16 KJV)

Trouble is, bottom line, most of the time; it's not someone else's fullness we want, but ours! We want it ourselves, come on, 'fess up, you want to feature. But the Holy Spirit cuts that ground from under our feet saying, "***In Him*** my darling, ***in Him*** dwells all the fullness of the Godhead bodily." (Colossians 2:9-14 NKJV)

Outside of that...you know it, zilch, nada, nothing.

We can't actually move on until we see this; the altogether ***other than us*** way, He is.

His thoughts aren't ours.

He is utterly different from us.

'*You are from beneath, I am from above*'. (Isaiah 55:8-9 NASB paraphrased).

That is the difference, this is where we collide with the Divine purpose, and this is where we learn to yield, to submit to the Higher Authority.

The cross is where His will and my will cross.

'***Thy** will be done*'...

That'll be it

[1] Thomas Monod.

# 10

# Road closed

We are all familiar with the heart-sink we experience when the sign ahead is, *'road works', 'road closed'* or something similar indicating a diversion of our route.

The result is usually frustration.

There's a five-mile detour to go half a mile.

When God starts to speak the route we determined to use we find, is marked - *'detour.'*

There's a detour we need to make.

We wants us to experience Him in a different way.

This is where we truly discover there is a collision of wills, of judgements, of purpose, a conflict of minds, of ideas, of perceptions, of values.

His way is not ours and we know it.

His view is altogether different from ours. (cf Isaiah 55:8-9).

The way He views situations, people, circumstances.

We protest.

It's nothing new - there was a collision in Jesus' day between the way He perceived things and the way the religious leaders viewed them; His disciples frequently didn't understand where He was coming from. They saw it one way He, completely differently.

In Luke 9 we see several instances where the disciples were totally bemused and confused by Jesus' responses, culminating in -

*"When it came close to the time for his Ascension, he gathered up his courage and steeled himself for the journey to Jerusalem. He sent messengers on ahead. They came to a Samaritan village to make arrangements for his hospitality. But when the Samaritans learned that his destination was Jerusalem, they refused hospitality.*

*When the disciples James and John learned of it, they said, "Master, do you want us to call a bolt of lightning down out of the sky and incinerate them?"*

*Jesus turned on them: "Of course not!" And they travelled on to another village."* (Luke 9:54-56 The Message)

He had a heavenly mind set; a mind set on doing the will of the Father.

They and we have an earthly one.

That's an illustration of our journey right there; they wanted to call down fire on these people. From the natural to the spiritual, the transformation mentioned in Romans 12:1-2. Being transformed in our thinking and perceiving.

During the course of your exploration of His ways you will frequently find Him saying things that just don't compute to your natural mind.

Sometimes you will consider what He asks absolute madness. It is as though He didn't realise the consequences.
But the insistence is there.

You cannot escape it.

It must be His way or no way.

Do the thing.

There is no reconciliation here; that old, earthly man must allow the heavenly man to take precedence. *'If anyone desires to come after Me, let him deny himself…and follow Me'* (Matthew 16: 24 – 26 NKJV) takes on a new meaning.

Deny yourself; your arguments; your preferences; your defence; your justifications for why you can't; your assessment of the situation; your judgement; your suspicion; your common sense – deny it.

Do the thing.

Exactly as He tells you.

We can never be sure we are doing the right thing unless we submit to Him; keep Him in that place of pre-eminence; and ourselves in that place of submission to His will and His Lordship.

Rendering Him first position, and us His love slaves.

He intends that we should have everything; He isn't second lining us, this is done to bring us into fullness, not to deny us.

He must have His place of absolute Lordship within us in order that we come into His fullness.

We come after Him in order to derive all the benefits, all the value, He places on us.

We aren't being repressed or squashed but following hard after.

Who worries about taking second place, if you get all the benefits of the Winner?

It is the only safe place to be and function from - in Him.

# 11

# You are late again Lord

In our humanity we are often prone to thinking that God is asleep or late.

Nothing is further from the truth - we are the ones who need to wake up and He is never late. He is the One who wrote -

*"Arise, you sleeper! Rise up from the dead and the Anointed One will shine his light into you!"* (Ephesians 5:14)

He isn't the One who needs to get His act together, wake up or move, we are the ones who need to do all three.

He might appear to be late in our timing or slow to move, but again, it all has to do with perception.

This is all about learning His ways, for example how to wait and wait well.

You can wait, but not wait well; if you are full of murmuring and complaining you are not waiting well and you are learning nothing - you are going to be in for a l.o.n.g. wait my friend!

Maybe we need to look at some people who have gone before us to learn from their mistakes.

Famous people, who got the right idea but missed it when it came to waiting for God's timing and His way.

You will see they just could not wait, both did what they thought best, with disastrous consequences. You can hear God beloved but miss Him in terms of timing.

There is always a test of your patience involved.

The tale of king Saul is a classic example.

Samuel had said, *"Wait until I arrive."* (1 Samuel 13:8 - 14 The Voice), Saul waits seven days then takes matters into his own hands.

But to test Saul's **obedience**, he hangs around a bit: **1 Samuel 15** tells the full story…

Saul falls victim to his own insecurities, feels *'impelled'* to act and as a result, loses the kingdom.

He took precipitate action.

It lost him the throne.

King David: he wants to get the ark back to Jerusalem; here his motive is right; his heart is right; his sense of God's purpose is right; but his method is out.

He gets so enthusiastic, carried away with his own ideas he forgets to follow the Maker's instructions on *how* the ark should be moved. Not so much about timing this one, but method.

Someone died as a result, and it was sometime later before the ark went back to where it belonged.

You can see that story in 2 Samuel 6.

What am I saying?

Keep in the place of prayer.

Make sure you know not only His request, but also His way and His timing.

Don't just get the instruction and run off with it.

Stay connected.

Do it His way.

He is the Head.

You are the body.

The body takes instructions from the head.

Wait for His timing.

Wait for His method.

Go when He says.

It's all about that lovely fruit of the Spirit – patience.

How's it working out for you?

# 12

# Pleasure and pain

*I walked a mile with Pleasure;*
*She chatted all the way;*
*But left me none the wiser*
*For all she had to say.*

*I walked a mile with Sorrow,*
*And ne'er a word said she;*
*But, oh! The things I learned from her,*
*When sorrow walked with me.*

This Robert Browning poem came to me today as we near the end of our time together.

Some twenty years ago Graham Cooke taught on something he called *'cycles of intimacy.'*

They went right across life; there was a relational cycle, a work cycle; a life cycle; a cycle of anointing; a cycle of transformation; everything was there.

In all these cycles the common thing he observed, was that we experienced pleasure and pain; weakness and power; achievement and suffering.

As we are currently exploring what experiencing God will look like, we cannot shrink from the things that we don't like, such as trials, pain, and difficulty.

Troubles will come; pain of one sort of another will accompany you on your way from time to time, but as Browning's poem says, it is sorrow and pain that teach us so much more than pleasure.

As much as we hate it, tribulation is the thing that teaches us the most, if we let it.

There's a brilliant book by Paul Bullheimer, *'Don't waste your sorrows'* - I recommend it if you are serious in your pursuit of God, because if you are set on following hard after Jesus, trials and tests you will discover, are a necessary part of your journey, your growth cycle.

Without them you will learn nothing.

Despite the look on your face, I can tell you, that is **good** news; very good news.

You need both tribulation and trials to work faith and patience in you - hear Peter on the subject -

1 Peter 4:12 NKJV

*'[Suffering for God's Glory] Beloved, do not think it strange concerning the fiery trial which is to try you, as though some strange thing happened to you;'*

He goes on to say why -

*'but rejoice to the extent that you partake of Christ's sufferings, that when His glory is revealed, you may also be glad with exceeding joy.'*

Those very trials mean you are **partakers** with Christ.

You cannot have all the good things He gives you without the accompanying suffering.

He's not some sort of celestial Santa Claus.

He calls you to be with Him in everything, the good, the bad and the ugly; and for His part guarantees that He will be with you too, in your difficult times.

That little bit of inconvenient enlightenment knocks a hole in the prosperity gospel and some.

You need not fear trouble when it comes beloved, because He will walk with you every step of the way, guiding you as is best for you.

You need not fear problems because every problem comes ready made with its provision.

These are the things you learn, that become flesh upon you, as you walk life's highway with Him.

This is what He means when He says He will *never* leave nor forsake you, (cf Hebrews 13:5).

Life happens and He will be there.

Sticking closer than a brother.

After the revelation comes the practical.

God loves to make what He has shown you real in your experience of Him, and the good news, the really good news, is that a trial or trouble actually opens the way for Him to be something *new* to you; something that He could never have been at any other time.

So, if you are in a pit right now, why not ask Him this question –

'*What do you want to be to me right now that you couldn't be at any other time?*'

The answer will delight you and cause you to have your very own **experience** of God.

So, relax and enjoy.

# 13

# The Comforter

Jesus promised He would send 'another' Comforter - someone just like Him.

Interesting word 'another'. 'Another' just like Me, he was saying in John's gospel, *'and when He comes He will lead you into all truth and…will bring to your recollection everything I have said'.*

Couldn't wish for more could we?

Someone who **is** like Jesus, exactly like Him, living inside us.

Our part is to walk with Him and experience Him.

Enjoy Him and grow in Him - it's the chief end of man, to glorify God and enjoy Him forever.

Not to argue with Him; walk with Him, agree with Him -

*'Can two walk together, unless they are agreed?'* (Amos 3:3 NKJV)

You can't argue with God the Holy Spirit beloved and hope to win.

He will outwit and out-wait you every single time.

And He will do it with a smile on His face.

Your problem now is - He's moved in.

And He's after intimacy.

Communion.

Union in fact.

No longer two wills, but one.

His.

He's here in Person.

If you fool yourself like Israel did and ask for someone with skin on, a *man* to rule over you, you could end up with a Saul, just as they did. The Lord said of them when He sent Samuel to them *'they have not rejected you but they have rejected Me'* (1 Samuel 8:7 NASB)

What an indictment.

God's chosen people.

Reject Him.

When push comes to shove - rejection is His portion.

Does He retaliate?

*'Father forgive them, they know not what they do...'* (Luke 23:34 KJV)

Your turned back and stiffened neck; your arched eyebrows and question - *'You want what?'* when He asks for that which you gave Him in a time of peace. Your desire to be king of your own life; your demand to have patience and can I have it *now*; never elicits anything but love and forgiveness from Him.

He knows what rebels we all are.

And He loves us.

Without condition.

But He won't leave us there.

The least we can do is recognise our own wilful nature, our desire to be our own king and repent.

Have another thought.

Turn.

Return.

To the lover of our souls.

In order to be healed, we must first accept we have a terminal condition.

The leprosy of sin, self-government - clings to us.

But there's a cure 100% guaranteed.

**1 John 1:9.**

He is faithful.

*'He has not dealt with us according to our sins…'* (Psalm 103:10 NKJV)

What a relief that is.

# 14

# The Executive Member

I sense we are not quite finished with the work of the Holy Spirit in our lives; that is, with understanding *why* He indwells us.

He hasn't come just so we can speak in tongues, prophesy and interpret dreams, those manifestations are the evidence that He indwells us. His job, His main task, is to conform us to the image of Jesus. So, you will find He will knock off everything that doesn't look like Him; remove every negative thing and replace it with Jesus, until the work is complete

Our part is simply to yield to Him -

[1] *'Still, still, without ceasing*
*I feel it increasing*
*This fervour of Holy desire*
*And often exclaim*
*Let me die in the flame*
*Of a love that can never expire!'*

A poem written by Madame Guyon, 'martyr to the Holy Spirit', as she was once described. She allowed such a deep work to be done in her inmost being that no-one around her understood where she was coming from. Least of all the religious leaders of her time…

But it was all the work of the Minister of the Interior.

The Holy Spirit.

He is the Executive Member of the Trinity.

God the Father is Spirit and unseen; Jesus the Son, the visible Member of the Godhead; the Holy Spirit is the Executive Member; the One who gets the job done. Madame Guyon's poem is a prayer I linger over *'let me die in the flame of Your love.'*

The flame of Your love.

The fire of the Holy Spirit burns for us, not against us.

It's just that.

Sometimes doesn't **feel** like it's burning *for* you when you are trying desperately to avoid the heat.

The ancients knew, those mystics of the 12 - 14th century - another of them would say *'Lord give me three wounds; the wound of contrition, the wound of compassion and the wound of seeking after You'*. Attributed to Julian of Norwich.

They knew a thing or two.

They kept the main thing the main thing.

They knew that this world and everything in it is passing away and only that which had eternal value would last, so they ensured they *'set their affections on things above, not on the earth below'*. That's a quote from the book of Colossians - I'll let you find it.

The Holy Spirit is in us to form Christ in us; and He isn't apologising.

*'His only design, your dross to consume and your gold to refine...'* as the old hymn has it. (George Keith, 'How firm a foundation ye saints of the Lord', Baptist hymnal 579.)

It's a slow process, a step-by-step, choice after choice lifestyle, to go the way of the Spirit not the way of the flesh.

But if you keep going with those choices...

Fulcrum point is eventually reached.

We tip over and the balance changes.

At last there is *'more of You Jesus, and less of me'* until we say *'all of You and none of me'.*

He must increase, I must decrease, to quote John the Baptist…

When this point is reached you will be of unconscious assistance to everyone who crosses your path.

Jesus in you is so powerful He will touch them.

His love for them will flow out from you.

And the *'Mighty miracles'*, of which He spoke, for example, in John 14:12 will become a reality.

And you, well you are aware of nothing but Him...you are too busy *'gazing on the crucified'*...that's an old hymn too as is this -

[2] *'All for Jesus! All for Jesus*
*All my being's ransomed powers;*
*All my thoughts and words and doings,*
*All my days and all my hours...'*

Sums up absolute yieldedness I'd say. Right there -

*'Let my hands perform His bidding;*
*Let my feet run in His ways;*
*Let mine eyes see Jesus only;*
*Let my lips speak forth His praise...*

*Since mine eyes were fixed on Jesus,*
*I've lost sight of all beside;*
*So enchained my spirit's vision,*
*Gazing on the Crucified...'*

That'll be it.

The Holy Spirit will have had His way with you.

Lovely.

And rest.

---

[1] *'The Fervour of Holy Desire'* 'The Christian book of Mystical' Verse
A W Tozer, et al Martino Publishing 2010, p 53
[2] *'All for Jesus'*, Mary D James, Redemption Hymnal 608

# 15

# Will you have Me?

For those who are still unsure, try this -

*'As many as are led by the Spirit of God, these are the sons of God'* (Romans 8:14 NKJV)

This isn't referring to the gifts of the Holy Spirit but to His leading in all things. It is referring to those who are **living** in the Spirit, by the Spirit, and being taught by Him daily.

His ways surely aren't our ways.

It is the Lord's doing.

Surely it is marvellous in our eyes!

But He's challenging us again.

To a one on one, walk with Him alone.

Chips are down.

Face to face.

Heart to heart.

Will you have **Me**?

Really experience **Me**?

Not your idea of Me.

Here's My cup, will you come and drink?

To have and to hold from this day forth, cleaving only to **Me**?

No matter how far we have gone, or think we have gone in our Christian walk, He presses this one thing, *'Have I been with you so long, and yet you have not known Me, Philip?'* (John 14:9 NKJV)

It is in this place, ground zero; we find everything we **thought** we knew about Christ is brought into the light of His countenance.

Under His scrutiny…

Ground zero.

*"That's where we need to start beloved"*, He says.

Right there, with your understanding of **Me**.

He did it all the time, with Nicodemus – a man of the law, he knew a thing or two...With the woman of Samaria, she thought she knew some things; the helpless cripple, 38 years in the same place, thought he knew what he needed; the man blind from birth; all started again from ground zero drinking from the well of water that would **never** run dry.

'*Without Me…'* (John 15:5 NKJV)

I know, don't rub it in, zilch, nada, nothing!

He will not touch the thing until it is beyond all human hope.

He's not healing the old man; He's making a new one.

After His image.

*'I Am the bread of life'* (John 6:35 NIV), there is nothing here in this world that can feed you, nothing in this world that can meet your need…

Bread of heaven or you're dead.

Life in the Spirit

*'Let My people go that they might worship **Me.**** (Exodus 7:16 NIV)

He demanded of Pharaoh.

Not let them go so that they are free to roam, but that they might worship **Me**.

He's always having to bring us back to Himself.

*'Lord, to whom shall we go? You have the words of eternal life…'* (John 6.68 NKJV)

So, what Pharaoh is holding you back from worshipping Him alone right now?

What Isaac do you still need to put on the altar?

Questions, questions.

Make you think though don't they…

# 16

# You are the God who sees me

Some of you will know where that comes from.

*'You are the God who sees me.'* (Genesis 16:13 NIV)

The story is found in Genesis 16, where we find a desperate Sarai suggesting Abram sleep with Hagar, her Egyptian maidservant to produce an heir.

The upshot is, you guessed it, the girl becomes pregnant and then, of course, she openly despises her mistress who is unable to conceive…

Sarai complains.

Abram passes the buck and tells Sarai to do as she thinks with the girl who ends up wandering in the desert - pregnant.

It is here beside a well, that Jesus makes an appearance - funny that, He does it again with a woman of Samaria - and has a conversation with her telling her not to be concerned, He promises to bless the child in her womb; a boy from whom a nation will come; and He tells her to call the child Ishmael - God hears.

As a result of this encounter, she calls the place where she sat Beer Lahai Roi, the well of the One who lives and sees me. (Genesis 16:13-14 KJV)

There she was in the middle of nowhere and He saw her…
Nothing changes.

We're in the middle of nowhere - and He sees us.

He searches us out and *we* discover He sees us; all the time;
everywhere.

We can run but we can't hide is the moral of this tale.

No matter how far we go or change our outward appearance;
change sex even; He sees.

*'You are the Living God who sees me'.*

So, question: why are you running this day?

What are you trying desperately to hide from Him right now?

Do you think you have committed the unforgivable sin for the
umpteenth time this week?

Or what has He been chasing you with?

What does He want to *give* you that you are reluctant to
receive?

Why are you fearful, Oh ye of little faith?

When He hunts us down and finds us under whatever pile of
dirt we are hiding, it isn't to condemn or chastise us, but to bless
us.

To cleanse us and lift us up.

He has nothing but good for us.

Circumstances may be bad; dire even, we've messed up - again!
But His intentions towards us are always good.

*'For I know the thoughts that I think toward you, says the Lord, thoughts of peace and not of evil, to give you a future and a hope. Then you will call upon Me and go and pray to Me, and I will listen to you. And you will seek Me and find Me, when you search for Me with all your heart. I will be found by you, says the Lord'* (Jeremiah 29:11-14 NKJV)

Jeremiah's message of hope to the captives in Babylon.

They were there because of their rebellion towards Him, but still He comes with the same message of restoration to us when we are captive to our own idea of Him -

*'I know the thoughts I have towards you and they are to bless and prosper you...'*

Israel are still in 'captivity' but He hasn't given up on them, He will restore their fortunes again in spite of everything they have done against Him.

Would He do any less for you who are His bride, His chosen one?

I leave you to think about that one.

# 17

# Draw me

The maiden in the Song of Songs asks for something very dangerous, she says, *'draw me'* and then she says, *'then we will run together'.* (Song of Solomon 1:4 NASB).

I wonder sometimes who put those words into her mouth, because Jesus said no-one comes except the Father draw them...

Everything starts with Him and ends with Him.

He is the beginning and the end.

Alpha and Omega.

We have looked at this principle numerous times on this journey together.

He initiates, we respond.

The Bridegroom initiates, the bride responds.

He invites us, we say *'Yes Lord'.*

*'Yes Lord, yes Lord, yes'* as the song says.

Can't say 'No' and 'Lord' in the same sentence.

We are responders to the Divine will... *Thy* Kingdom come.

We have to get this firmly in our thinking; He is the Holy One of Israel, we are the sheep of His pasture; He initiates, we respond…

He asks us to join Him, not the other way around.

We are co-workers with Him in the lead.

We join Him, not the other way around.

We looked at it in the session *'This way up'* and again in *'Mind the Gap'* but of course, the human condition is short-term memory loss; we constantly forget, so we need a gentle reminder from time to time.

We just keep forgetting that He is the Creator and we the created; we bow the knee to Him, not He to us; He asks we say 'yes'; so many changes in our world view it clean takes your breath away.

He asks us to be totally dependent on Him not on ourselves or others.

He asks us to give rather than receive.

To die to ourselves that others may live.

Totally upside down.

But that's the kingdom.

Its value system is completely other than - remember instead of privacy, He wants authenticity and openness; instead of material success, He calls for sacrifice; instead of convenience and comfort, put the other fellow first.

That will distort your life for a start if you begin to practice it.

If that isn't upside down in this present darkness, I don't know what is.

But there you are, you signed up for this, so it must be His way or no way.

How's it working out for you?

# 18

# There may be trouble ahead

A 'golden oldie' again.

*"There may be trouble ahead, but while there's music and moonlight and love and romance, let's face the music and dance..."*[1]

Facing the music.

Another thought.

We used to call it that when we were going to be corrected by someone - we were going to 'face the music'.

Correction beloved; is not rejection. But to hear the reaction of some Christians to it, correction that is, you could think that they were experiencing rejection. The moment the warm fuzzy is removed and the dummy is taken out of their mouths, the yell goes up.

The decibel level increases.

God is getting serious with them; He's looking for them to grow up; to mature.

So, He's asking for a degree of discipline in their lives. He isn't getting it.

Why is it that some of us will not submit to even a modicum of discipline in our lives?

Answering my own question, it could be our arch enemy, self; in the form of self-will.

We have this value system we have created over the years by which we measure everything, and if what is asked of us no - matter **who** does the asking - we perceive and receive it as criticism, rejection, or even judgement.

We are shooting ourselves in the foot.

I wouldn't be describing you would I?

Would I?

Oh dear.

It is time my darling, to face the music and dance with Him, as the old song went.

You won't win this one you know.

You're just wasting the only commodity you have.

Time.

You can't get it back.

Why not capitulate and do as He asks?

There's a good soul; I knew you would be open to reason.

[1] Lyricfind. Composer Seth Macfarlane/sung by Fred Astaire.

# 19

# One Master

These last few messages could be described as revisions so let's take a look.

1. The Holy Spirit's ministry of the interior is unceasing.

2. His Majesty is in us both to will and to do.

3. It requires our co-operation.

4. If we allow Him, He will work His great work of sanctification in us in such a way that the world and its attractions become very distant indeed.

Like the maiden in the Song of Songs, who finds herself in a journey from initial love to mature love we will trace our journey into His great heart of love for us and come to the place where we desire His will.

We only want to work where we see He is working and where He invites us to join Him.

All our ambition lies in the dust.

Agendas likewise.

And there is nothing but loyalty to Him.

Loyalty to that One Master.

Sometimes God appears to withdraw.

One minute we are basking in His presence.

We can take the world on singlehanded.

The next, we are like Joseph, down a pit; darkness; misery, where did it all go?

It's part of the training.

What we are experiencing is He is moving us from feeling to faith.

You know about the three cats of course?

No?

Three cats were walking along a wall, one in front was called Fact, next one, Faith, and the third, Feeling.

All the time Faith kept his eyes on Fact he was all right. When He looked around at Feeling they both fell off the wall.

Point?

Don't look at or live in your feelings.

He gives us an experience of Himself and just as we are set to camp there, enjoying the experience; we're saying like Peter on the mount of transfiguration *'shall we build three tabernacles?'* (Matthew 17:1-4 NKJV), He moves the scenery, and it all goes dark.

Very dark.

Now He want us to learn to live not by feelings; the next meeting; the next conference; the next word; the next encounter; the next laying on of hands - but faith.
Raw faith. God says it; I believe it that settles it.

Faith.

The substance of things hoped for, the evidence of things not seen... (Hebrews 11:1 KJV)

Uh huh.

Not so good.

It is here we learn that the valley is the place where we grow, not the mountaintop.

We can't live on mountaintop experiences.

Ask Pete.

He wanted to camp there.

We have to have that most recent experience of Him taken away so that He can give us something better, something more of Himself.

An absolutely cast-iron certainty that He is as He says He is - whether we *feel* it or not.

Hope.

Steadfast and certain.

Whether the situation changes or not.

It doesn't matter.
We trust Him.

Forsaking
All
I
Trust
Him

F.A.I.T.H.

That testing time has to come.

After manifestation, comes hiddenness.

Sure as night follows day.

Ah.

Light first.

Followed by darkness.

He's done it before.

Now we see.

Perfect submission, all is at rest.

*'Lord, I trust you. I don't understand, but I trust you.'*

He loves that.

# 20

# Trials

1 Peter 4:12–15 NKJV – *'Don't think it strange when trials come'*. They are really important because you are now experiencing Him - for real. They are not there just to *get* through somehow, but to *grow* through. That's what they are for.

That you may **grow**.

Mature.

That word again - maturity.

Lack nothing.

God is seeking to establish certain core character traits and values in you.

So that you rejoice in suffering, tribulation, and rejection.

Bless when you are persecuted and reproached; and when evil is spoken of you, you respond in the opposite spirit.

You don't give like for like.

Punch for punch.

You are under God's training, in His school.

It's sometimes simply about learning the art of *enduring* under trial.

Some tests are over more quickly than others.

Maybe they are allowed to teach you patience.

That's the purpose of trouble.

*"Tribulation works .........."* fill in the blank, you can do it.

Demonic oppression is there to teach you about **power**.

Human opposition teaches you **grace** – so that your response might be gracious at all times and in all circumstances.

Tension and difficulty are there to teach you to **rest**.

And trouble - well we know what that one is there for. Clue - it starts with the letter 'p', like tribulation.

Endurance is a constant in this; you can't duck out or be rescued because you will have to go around that test again, and again, and again, until He is satisfied. He's saying, *'let Me grow these lovely attributes in you power, grace, rest and peace - stick with the process sweetheart, and you will become like My Son.'*

We never develop the character He wants to bestow upon us if we lose our grip on the maturity, He is holding out to us.

Patient endurance under trial.

Wouldn't that be a place to come to instead of looking for the nearest fire exit?

*"Endure hardness as a good soldier"*, Paul says to Timothy (2 Timothy 2:3,4 NKJV)

Here we are with something else then.

Hardness.

No thank you!

But it's all part of the training.

Like fortitude.

We are an army.

In training.

Three steps here: training ground; proving ground and finally; battle ground.

Don't have time to get bored do you?

We could be on manoeuvres tomorrow.

That'll sort the men out from the boys and some.

# 21

# Two pathways

Sometimes we need to stop and look at how far we have come and where we are headed.

Mountain climbing is not for the unprepared or ill equipped.

Patient endurance, perseverance and fortitude are keys. Without them you will only climb a few hills in God, you'll never climb mountains.

Choices again.

*'What man building a tower doesn't sit down and work out the cost?'*

Jesus I think.

Time to slow down again and recap.

Think really carefully about the next leg of the journey.

Take a look at what we have seen so far travelling with Jesus through His Sermon on the Mount.

It's not for the faint hearted.

Those with wishbone, not backbone.

God is gracious.

He constantly stops and invites us to choose.

He won't love us any the less if we don't go on.

We always know where we are with Him, but we never know what He is going to do next; that's the problem, not knowing. But He's looking for maturity.

Where you trust Him *without* knowing.

Where you do things differently.

You think differently.

Out of step with others perhaps.

They won't understand from here on up.

Very few will walk with you, and if they do they won't say much.

Time to take stock beloved.

It isn't going to get any easier.

We are heading for higher ground.

The atmosphere will thin.

Breathing will become difficult.

You may sense the beginning of altitude sickness...

No disgrace.

He loves you just the same whether you stop now or go on.

Congratulations on getting this far. Now you need His wisdom to respond to what He is teaching you and where He wants to take you. He's turned you from enjoyment to endurance, and the scenery has completely changed.

From church to Kingdom.

Not many of those who started out with you are still there.

You can't cast out the cross and crucify the devil. You must embrace the cross and cast out the enemy of your soul.

Submit to God, *'you are My Friends if you do whatever I command you'*... (John 15:14 NIV)

Suddenly we find we have moved around that circle we talked about to - friendship.

Here we find that there is no such thing as a casual friendship with God, no matter what people may say.

There are no *casual* friends in the Kingdom.

God is intentional.

Intentional.

He would like you to be the same, but He never forces you.

The work of God here in endurance is to produce, vulnerability and submission.

Surrender.

Not partial.

A place where you become so vulnerable you have no confidence in yourself at all; only in Him.

*Then* He will take your confidence to a high place.

But it's that altitude thing again.

Are you really up for the next part of the climb?

Let's rest here a while so you can think about the next stage of your journey where you will learn to communicate only with Him, with the Holy Spirit as your guide.

There are two pathways you see.

The road divides here.

One is the path with lots of people, plenty of chat and interaction, doing things together. The other is just you and Him, walking into a life less ordinary - the Kingdom.

This path is not well trodden, it is overgrown. You enter it alone, on your knees.

And you only hear one voice.

His.

You choose.

# 22

# Weakness

*'I can't...'*

The whole point of weakness is that He brings you to a place of vulnerability, insecurity, and inadequacy.

Perfect.

So far as He is concerned.

Uncomfortable.

For you.

Extremely.

Perfect for Him though.

He can move in.

He isn't going to make you strong, don't ask for it.

That needs to be settled.

He's never going to give you something that will keep you at a distance from Him or not totally dependent upon Him.

He is going to *be* your strength and your all sufficiency.

From now on He's going to *be* for you everything you need.

Your insecurity and inability are His opportunity.

Nice one.

He's making you weak so that you develop submission, patience, dependence, perseverance, endurance, fortitude, faith, grace, mercy, humility, and gratitude...all those lovely things.

Oh my.

You become so grateful that you are no longer strong but weak.

No longer self-confident.

But leaning on the Beloved.

Now you sing with the joy of the Lord when you are in difficulties, and you thank Him because you know He is right there with you in the midst of it all.

Now you *know* that for every problem there is provision.

So you wait confidently *'I know You; it's here somewhere I'll just wait here until I see it.'*

You're confident.

You stop trying to escape.

And trade it for another 'e' word -

Embrace.

You embrace the cross with joy, knowing Christ is being formed in you.

His Majesty.

You rejoice when you see your old man being killed off, you're no longer screaming to be delivered but jumping for joy at the relief of walking in the Spirit not in the flesh or your carnal nature.

You can really begin to say *'The essence of this new life is no longer mine for the Anointed One lives His life through me - we live in union as one'.* (Galatians 2:20)

And know this is increasingly the truth.

After the cross comes resurrection life.

Christ is formed in you.

Resurrection life springs forth from you.

Rivers of living water flow from you, refreshing others.

As you love them as He does.

You see everything from His perspective.

You receive the wisdom that comes from above in this life.

Reigning over yourself and your circumstances, you put the enemy to flight.

Your name is known in hell.

Your flesh is under control.

You are walking with the Lamb.

You're getting the hang of it; there is a place in God reserved for you marked out by the claim pegs of victory, that He wants you to have, that will make others say you are so way out you'll never get back.

Indeed!

Absolutely right.

This is the place of breakthrough and follow through; you are no longer a follower or a believer, but a disciple, you are *continuing* with Him. Now you no longer have a breakthrough and lose it, you have the strength to follow through. You are truly living from heaven to earth not the other way around; and it was worth it all, all the trials and the tribulations. You wouldn't change one of them. Now you lead others in the same way you have gone, helping them to breakthrough, follow through and continue following hard after your Lord and Master, Jesus.

There is a place here where the mysteries hidden in God are being revealed to you...now, He calls you 'friend'.

You call yourself His love slave.

That circle we talked about is nearly complete - this time around anyway.

# 23

# The love slave

Comes the time then, when you are so in love with Him that you ask if you can be His love slave; you ask Him to pierce your ear as the slave who loved the Master and didn't want to go free, and that you *'may dwell in the house of the Lord forever, and behold His beauty'* (Psalm 27:4 NKJV)

Paul often described himself as a prisoner, or love slave of Jesus Christ.

It seems to relate to the power of the conversion experience.

For me, it was a complete turnaround, just like Paul – *'I was like that, now I am like this'.*

'He who is forgiven much, loves much'. (Paraphrase Luke 7:47), the woman caught in adultery. I so identified with this woman; still do. I have no difficulty in being His love slave.

But it isn't the same for everyone.

Many struggle with the steps we have already taken through sonship, servanthood, friendship and finally the one we are looking at just now…love slave. I know no easy answer, except to pray for the grace of yielding.

We do not know what rebels we are until we are asked to lay down our own plans and surrender to Someone else, even if that Someone else is the Lord Jesus Christ.

So how is it working out for you? Have you enjoyed reading these sessions and made a mental assent but know in your heart if He were to ask the ultimate of you, that you put your Isaac on the altar, you would not be able to part with him, or it, whatever constitutes your particular Isaac.

There is no shame my darling, no disgrace.

There are no exams to pass, no grades to win.

It is all an affair of the heart.

The Father is looking for a Bride for His Son.

One who will love Him.

She is destined for the throne.

To reign and rule with Him for eternity.

Whatever you choose, you will reign and rule, but maybe not to the level you could have.

Decisions as we saw very early on, determine destiny. Attitudes determine altitude.

He is not going to love you any the less.

But it isn't too late to put your whole self in.

Not just an arm or a leg.

It's never too late with Him.

He is the God of the second, third, and fourth, and more, chances.

What happens is we run out of time.

If we procrastinate out of fear, or whatever, we just run out of the time it will take Him to prepare us for the best He has for us.

But the choice is always ours.

Measure or abundance.

No disgrace.

No shame.

No judgement.

Tomorrow we are going to look a little more closely at what God is aiming at.

See you then.

# 24

# On making mistakes

Have you ever given any thought to what Jesus might ask you on the day when the rewards are handed out? I heard something of Graham Cooke's recently and was arrested by his question - are you living in measure or abundance?

I wasn't sure.

But one thing I am sure about is that I am striving to live in abundance not measure or I would make the exchange Jesus bought for me less than He intended, and I don't want that.

I want **everything** God has planned for me.

All of it.

And that's gratitude, not greed.

I know He has a territory staked out with the claim pegs of victory already prepared for me to walk in, I've already referred to it. So I keep on keeping on, sometimes with the face of an ox, head down and persevering; the Christian has four faces you know: of a human, a lion, an ox, and an eagle (Ezekiel 1:10 NIV)

I don't want to get there and hear Him say, as He gestures to pictures of me doing things I had never done, *'I had all this for you, but you didn't press in and receive them...'* you didn't persevere...

My first pastor told the story of two grand staircases with pictures going up the walls on either side and it was a similar illustration, the road we walk and the road God has prepared for us.

Did you know there are two paths you can take?

The high road or the low road?

The path of passivity, the 'I can't' is the low road where you come into very little that He has planned; the way of abundance is the high road, where you gain all the territory He won for you on the cross.

Some of us, when we try something for the first time, and it goes wrong, never go there again.

That is the road to measure.

You paint yourself into a corner because you are so nervous to make a mistake and *'get it wrong'*.

A man who never made a mistake never made anything; you have yet to learn that with God, there *is* no such thing as getting it right or wrong; this is relational, you are in His school under His training; for His time; you *don't* know how to do this thing, that's why you are here.

Mistakes are how we learn.

He's factors them in.

We just tripped over your pride, that's all, right there…

You thought you should know, and you are disappointed with yourself that you didn't and in your estimation, you got it wrong. *'Silly dove',* as God said of Ephraim. (Hosea 7:11 KJV)

When we do something for the first time, we are **always** going to make mistakes. Live with it. Without making mistakes you will never grow.

The first time I ever cooked a meal for my new husband, I made a number of mistakes, but I didn't stop trying until I had mastered the art, and he didn't die of starvation waiting for me to get it right.

Simple illustration but you get what I mean.

So, question, are you aiming for abundance or measure?

And do you want to change your mind and start really meaning business with God from this point on?

Never too late, just be prepared to learn and in that learning process, make some mistakes…

# 25

# The Cross

Jesus is altogether *'other than'* us in the way He looks at situations, people, and circumstances. If you followed the teaching from the *'School of the Spirit'*, you will know what I am talking about.

The fact is, wherever we look, we discover there is a clash of purpose and wills between Jesus and us.

A clash of judgements, a clash of purpose, a clash of minds, a clash of ideas, a clash of perceptions, a clash of values…clash, clash, clash.

We are discovering the reality of the application of the cross to our lives, and there's a clash of wills - mine versus His. We say freely enough *'Thy will be done'* but when it starts something in us kicks off.

It isn't new.

Jesus always has this effect.

Two value systems are colliding.

Just look again at the Gospels, there was a clash between Jesus and the religious leaders, and He clashed with His disciples – frequently. They thought one thing, He thought something completely different - they didn't like it.

He has a heavenly mind.

They and we have an earthly one.

That's our journey right there.

The journey of transformation that **Romans 12:1,2** talks about.

Being transformed in our *minds*.

During our journey together you will have noticed Him saying things that just don't compute to your natural mind.

Sometimes the *'other-than'* inside you is insisting on a certain course of action that you consider absolute madness!

But the insistence is there.

Do the thing.

Whatever it is.

You cannot escape it.

It must be this way or no way.

Do the thing.

There is no reconciliation here; that old, earthly man must allow the new, heavenly man, to take precedence.

*'If any man will come after Me let him deny himself and follow Me'* (Matthew 16:24 NKJV) takes on a whole new meaning. Like - deny yourself; your arguments; your reasoning; your justifications for why you can't do something; your assessment of the situation; your judgement; your suspicion; your common sense – deny it.

Do the thing.

Just as He tells you.

We can never be sure we are doing the right thing unless we submit to Him; keep Him in that place of pre-eminence; ourselves in that place of submission to His Lordship.

Rendering Him first position, and us His love slaves.

He intends that we should have everything; He wants us to have abundance, not measure; He isn't second lining us, all this is to bring us into fullness, into abundance, not deny us.

But He must have His place of absolute Lordship. We come after Him to derive all the benefits, all the value, He places on us, and won for us. We are not being repressed or squashed but following hard after Him.

Who minds taking second place if you get all that comes to the One in first place?

It's the only safe place to be.

*Available from Amazon.co.uk.

# 26

# Union with God

There are some who think that **union** with God is not possible in this life.

We aren't talking about something physical but spiritual here; deep calling to deep; spiritual union where two wills are united in common purpose and thought -

*'I and My Father are One.'*

*'I promised you to one Bridegroom, to Christ'.*

The moment we receive Jesus as our Lord and Saviour we receive all we need to live and enjoy the Christian life.

Jesus in us is the fullness of God.

We are in Him, He is in us, and He is in the Father.

Double wrapped.

The journey has just begun.

The journey to complete possession.

His of you.

*'I am my Beloved's and His desire is towards me…'*
So says the maiden at the end of the Song of Songs.

She has come on a journey into the heart of the Beloved.

She started out declaring she possessed Him –

*'My Beloved is mine and I am His'...*

She ends, knowing she belongs to Him and no other.

She has dropped her claim to possess Him and allows Him to possess her completely.

No wonder we see the parallel of marriage so often in scripture – the two shall become one.

That is what God is after, that two shall become one.

You, melded into one, Him.

Where does He start and where do you end?

You have walked into the glory and been swallowed up in the brilliance.

No longer two lives to be lived, but one.

His.

Through you.

And you are more than content to have it so.

Someone asked Georgian Banov what he was speaking on one evening and he was heard to say *'I don't know, I am a dead man'.*

No more opinions.

All is Him.

Seeing as He sees.

Speaking what He wants to say.

That sounds familiar…**John 4:34.**

Of course, that's what it is all about whilst we are here, doing what the Father wills. On earth as it is in heaven - can't get away from that it. We must be about our Father's business, just the same as Jesus was and He wasn't referring to His dad being a carpenter.

[1] *'Oh to be like Thee blessed Redeemer, this is my constant longing and prayer…'*

But there's only one way to do it.

Total consecration.

No longer two lives to be lived but one.

The anointing, the indwelling Presence, takes everything out of our hands.

I'm going to ask you some questions shortly. Questions, you know, are designed to transform your relationship and your walk with the Lord. A good teacher does their job best by questioning the pupils, making them *think* about what they really know and say they believe. Questions are designed to transform your understanding of yourself and how you are changing on this journey of discovery.

It's not just about your understanding something more about Jesus.

You have to **see** yourself in a new way.

The way He sees you - brilliant.

That's how He sees you.

So, how's it working out for you?

How are you doing?

How do you see yourself now compared with when we started this journey?

How do you see and relate to Him now?

I'll leave you with these...take your time, journal your answers.

---

[1] *'O to be like Thee, blessed Redeemer'* T. O. Chisholm, Redemption Hymnal Number 412

# 27

# It seems good

Paul says (Acts 15:28 KJV), *'it seemed good to me and the Holy Spirit'* and he goes on to say he wants to visit somewhere. Today it seems good to me to share with you a prayer I pray every day, it isn't long, but it does pack a certain punch. It goes like this:

*"Thank You Father it is You who schedule my conflicts.*

*Thank You Father, you have given me all the rights of an overcomer, more than a conqueror.*

*Thank You I am amongst wolves, but the Lion is padding alongside.*

*Thank You for this training ground.*

*Thank You I am in a new season, a new beginning.*

*Thank You that all I experience is for my good; for my profit; my increase; my training; my upgrade; my equipping…*

*I say 'Yes' to this development and embrace the joy and the pain.*

*Thank You my goal is greater faith and a more overtly supernatural lifestyle.*

*Thank You, you rightly correct me. (Jeremiah 46:28)*

*I trust You.*
*I love You.*

*Amen"*

I find I have been praying that daily since August 2009.

What am I saying?

There are times when we need to keep on praying things, not for God's benefit, but **ours** because when I pray that I am reinforcing what I want to become and where I want to go in Him. I am making sense of what is happening in my life. I have to remind myself that He is the author of my current area of conflict.

I am matching His intentional desires towards me with mine to be as He wants me to be. We are agreed and walking together (Amos 3:3 NKJV)

He wants us to grow; He is always present future with us; He always calls us higher.

Why not write a prayer of your own; something that reflects what you are becoming - an overcomer who is more than a conqueror?

Just a thought.

# 28

# Special consideration

There's an old hymn that contains the line: [1] *'His only design our dross to consume and our gold to refine.'*

God is a refiner, a purifier.

He puts us in hot situations to burn off the dross so that the pure gold of His Son can come forth in us. Not something we enjoy, but the result is well worth a little passing discomfort, unless of course you aren't interested in what happens in eternity.

God plans for that you see.

He plans for eternity.

That time when you and He will be one and you will reign and rule with Him according to what you have done with your time here.

Now there's a thought.

You aren't just in God's waiting room with your ticket to heaven secure in your baggage. What if when we get there you are simply asked why you didn't press into everything He wanted to give you?

I talked about it before.

No condemnation, just a question.

There's measure and there's fullness available.

I sense I need to press this issue.

There's measure and there's abundance, available.

There's 30, 60, 100 fold.

Available.

It's up for grabs.

Remember the two pathways and the two staircases?

He never forces or coerces us; He always gently leads us - that is if we are willing to follow.

He's always asking us if we want more of Him.

Doesn't compute to the religious mind.

But it does to those in an intimate relationship with Him; or those who desire it.

He's offering it to you again today – *'there's much more you can have you know.'*

The Kingdom - I have given it to you; *'Son, all I have is yours'.* (Luke 15:31 NKJV)

Will you receive it?

Will you come into everything I planned you should have from before the foundation of the earth?

It is possibly time to forget everything you have understood up to this point and launch yourself into an adventure so great, so vast, so blue, so You…

The possibilities are limitless.

You remember that poem too, don't you?

Limitless possibilities.

You serve a God and Father who is not only willing but eager for you to have everything He is and has. That must arouse a modicum of passion in you.

If not, perhaps this will; it is an extract from a prophetic word in Graham Cooke's CD series *'Favour'*:

*"It is My intention to personalise my grace in such a way that you become empowered in specific areas of your life so that rapid growth is the norm. I give you favour so that you may know that you have special consideration for My intentional desire to take place, even in the ordinary things of life.*

*I am indulging Myself so that you will become highly confident towards Me.*

*Look to Me. Look to Me. Look to Me. I have given you permission to dream and to make request for specific issues, problems, situations, and circumstances.*

*Favour is now being actively promoted by the Holy Spirit and equally contested by the enemy.*

*Favour is permission to ask, seek and knock in the sure and certain knowledge that God will say 'yes'.*

*Your life therefore, it about getting to 'Yes'. I will take your favour into a high and deep place of confidence in My goodness so that a greater faith anointing can begin to grow in you.*

*In this place of My indulgence, I will teach you to stand in the place of My desire. Your favour means you will stand in My presence and hear My heart saying 'yes'.*

*I will teach you to make a new beginning in the place of My victory over the enemy of your soul. I will develop in you the capacity to receive favour from people around you. You will come to bask in My desire for you. I will indulge Myself in your heart, your mind and your life. My desires shall be made known and they shall become your dreams."*

I'll leave you with that thought.

You could just have experienced God, right there, right then.

Why not take a few moments to write out that prophecy because it is for you.

Then you can think and pray about it, because it's for you beloved; for you.

---

[1] *'How firm a foundation'* Keith, Baptist Hymnal.

# 29

# Different

So, God doesn't want you to stay the same as you are right now; He has a vision of you becoming something much greater. He said of Abram *'Shall I tell him what I am about to do seeing he is going to become...'* (Genesis 18:17 NKJV paraphrase.)

Because Abe was going to father a nation and God saw that in the future, He spoke to Abram in the present as though he were already living in the future.

God is always present/future with us.

He doesn't visit us in our muck and misery of the past; He's dealt with all that; nor does He stand in the present, He speaks to what *He* sees.

The finished article.

It's called prophecy.

He wants to change *you*, by His Spirit, into a different man, a different woman.

To do that a prerequisite is that you come into alignment with His view of you.

That you agree with Him - *'Yes Lord; You've said it, I believe it'.*

You agree you are the head, not the tail.

You agree, you do not suffer from low self-esteem - whatever that may be.

You agree, you are more than a conqueror through Christ.

You are an overcomer.

You are predestined to reign and rule with Him.

You are His delight.

You are His passion.

You are **HIS** treasured possession.

Ah.

His.

His woman.

His Bride.

His beloved on whom His favour rests…

A thought right there, what would it be like to live every day understanding you were in the favour of God simply because He says so.

His beloved on whom His favour rests.

How silly would it be not to take advantage of that?

The One who created everything; Who owns everything: is saying *'ask and it will be given to you'*. (Matthew 7:7 NKJV)

You just won the lottery and no-one told you!

Favour.

Favourite.

That'll be you.

His favourite.

Step into it.

All He has for you.

You'll find that abundance we talked about is right there.

# 30

# Going up going on

*'There is no stopping in the Spirit filled life'* so, I understand, said one Smith Wigglesworth last century.

Question: have you stopped?

Stopped going up and going on I mean.

You'll know if you have.

Sat down.

Dropped out.

Disillusioned.

Fallen by the wayside.
Given up.

Offended?

God comes seeking those who for whatever reason have given up the race; or perhaps never really started. They got religion not relationship and of course, they got bored and fell away; or people upset them and that was that.

Your trouble probably was that you never actually experienced *Him*, you experienced people.

You were familiar with church and religion, but Jesus - He was someone far off.

What you lacked was an experience of Him.

A man with an experience, it is said, is beyond reason.

He wants you to experience Him for yourself.

My experience of Him won't cut it for you.

You need your own, personal, revelation.

That the God who knows you best, loves you best.

He has so much in store for you; His heart burns with the desire to give Himself to you in His fullness, that's why Jesus died.

To give you an **experience** of a life less ordinary.

A life lived in abundance, not measure.

Because every day you **experience** Him.

You expect Him at every turn to do something wonderful - simply because He is wonderful.

You wake every morning expectant. *'What are You going to do today Lord? I want to be part of that; experience You in it; love You in it; worship You in it'.*

What a partnership.

One with God and you are always in the majority.

He wants to give you Himself, e**verything** He is and everything He has, so that you will be wonderful too. And you will know it. And live like it.

If you have stopped, slowed down or fallen by the wayside, time to *'pick yourself up, dust yourself off and start all over again'* [1] as the old song goes.

Just make sure you start from a different place; a different perspective of just Who God is; and who you are; that you recognise how much He longs over you; that He loves you in just the same way as He loves His Son Jesus, because you are in Him; that you are the beloved of God on whom His favour rests.

You probably dropped back anyway because of what you knew of church, people, and experience, not really because you found anything missing in Him, because try as you will, you won't.

Find anything lacking in Him that is.

Remember -

*"Eternal life means to know and experience you as the only true God, and to know and experience Jesus Christ, as the Son whom you have sent."* (John 17:3)

That'll be it.

Experiencing God.

That's what it's all about.

Knowing Him and having a *real* experience of Him.

Go on, have another try.

You won't be disappointed.

Guaranteed.

[1] Nat King Cole

# 31

# The beginning

I was going to title this 'The End' but I realised it is far from that, it is actually just the beginning.

We have travelled together through the Sermon on the Mount, and I have spoken to you from my own personal experience of the Father, Jesus and the Holy Spirit. For me it seems incredible that when we launched on this journey together, I thought I was just going to jot down a few ideas about the Sermon, but Father had other ideas.

He has said I need to wind this one up now; the reason being I need to spend some quality time with Him myself now for a month or so at least. I have learned that you cannot keep giving out without filling up first. And it's my time now to spend some quality time in the secret place…I am *so* looking forward to it.

Time to sign out then, *'beloved, keep yourselves in the love of God'* - **Jude 21**.

Beryl M
15<sup>th</sup> December 2022

Other books in the series
'Thy Kingdom Come':

Living a Kingdom Lifestyle Volume 1
High, Higher, Highest Volume 2
Destined for the Throne Volume 3
From here to Eternity Volume 4

Other books by the same author:
School of the Spirit
He calls her Bride
The Divine Exchange

Printed in Great Britain
by Amazon

33563041R00169